THE SEXUAL LIFE
OF CATHERINE M.

Catherine Millet

Translated by Adriana Hunter

CORGI BOOKS

THE SEXUAL LIFE OF CATHERINE M.
A CORGI BOOK: 0 552 77172 4

Originally published by Editions du Seuil
First published in this English language edition by Serpent's Tail

PRINTING HISTORY
Editions du Seuil edition published 2001
Serpent's Tail edition published 2002
Corgi edition published 2003

5 7 9 10 8 6

Set in 11/13pt Sabon by
Falcon Oast Graphic Art Ltd.

Corgi Books are published by Transworld Publishers,
61–63 Uxbridge Road, London W5 5SA,
a division of The Random House Group Ltd,
in Australia by Random House Australia (Pty) Ltd,
20 Alfred Street, Milsons Point, Sydney, NSW 2061, Australia,
in New Zealand by Random House New Zealand Ltd,
18 Poland Road, Glenfield, Auckland 10, New Zealand
and in South Africa by Random House (Pty) Ltd,
Endulini, 5a Jubilee Road, Parktown 2193, South Africa.

Printed and bound in Great Britain by
Cox & Wyman Ltd, Reading, Berkshire.

Contents

1. Numbers

As a child I thought about numbers a great deal. The memories we have of single thoughts and actions we had in the first few years of life are very clear cut: they provide the first opportunities for self-awareness, whereas events shared with other people can never be isolated from the feelings (of admiration, fear, love or loathing) that those others inspire in us, feelings which, as children, we are far less able to identify or even understand. I, therefore, have particularly vivid memories of the thoughts which steered me into scrupulous counting exercises every evening before I went to sleep. Shortly after my brother was born (when I was three and a half), my family moved into a new apartment. For the first few years that we lived there, my bed was in the largest room, facing the door. I would lie staring at the light which came across the corridor from the kitchen where my mother and grandmother were still busying themselves, and I could never get to sleep until I had visualised these numerical problems one after the other. One of these problems related to the question of having several husbands. Not the possibility of the situation arising, which seems to have been accepted, but on the circumstances themselves. Could a woman have several husbands at the same time, or only one after the

11

other? In which case, how long did she have to stay married to each one before she could change? What would be an 'acceptable' number of husbands: a few, say five or six, or many more than that, countless husbands? How would I go about it when I grew up?

As the years went by, counting husbands was substituted for counting children. I imagine that, finding myself under the seductive spell of some identified man (in turns, a film star, a first cousin, etc.) and focusing my wandering thoughts on his features, I perhaps felt less uncertainty about the future. I could envisage in more concrete terms my life as a married young woman, and therefore the presence of children. More or less the same questions were raised again: was six the most 'acceptable' number or could you have more? What sort of age gap should there be between them? And then there was the ratio of girls to boys.

I cannot think back to these ideas without connecting them to other obsessions which preoccupied me at the same time. I had established a relationship with God which meant that every evening I had to think about what he was going to eat, so that the enumeration of the various dishes and glasses of water which I offered him mentally – fussing over the size of the helpings, the rate at which they were served, etc. – alternated with the interrogations into the extent to which my future life would be filled with husbands and children. I was very religious, and it could well be that my confused perception of the identities of God and his son favoured my inclination to counting. God was the thundering voice which brought men back into line without revealing himself to them. But I had been taught that he was also, and simultaneously,

the naked baby made of pink plaster which I put into the Christmas crib every year, the suffering man nailed to the crucifix before which we prayed – even though both of them were actually his son – as well as a sort of ghost called the Holy Spirit. Of course, I knew perfectly well that Joseph was Mary's husband, and that Jesus, even though he was both God and the son of God, called him 'Father'. The Virgin was indeed the mother of the Christ child, but there were times when she was referred to as his daughter.

When I was old enough to go to Sunday school, I asked to speak to the priest one day. The problem I laid before him was this: I wanted to become a nun, to be a 'bride of Christ', and to become a missionary in an Africa seething with destitute peoples, but I also wanted to have husbands and children. The priest was a laconic man, and he cut short the conversation, believing that my concerns were premature.

Until the idea of this book came to me I had never really thought about my sexuality very much. I did, however, realise that I had had multiple partners early on which is unusual, especially for girls, or it certainly was in the milieu in which I was brought up. I lost my virginity when I was eighteen – which is not especially early – but I had group sex for the first time in the weeks immediately after my deflowering. On that occasion I was obviously not the one who took the initiative in the situation, but I was the one who precipitated it – something I still cannot explain to myself. I have always thought that circumstances just happened to mean that I met men who liked to make love in groups or liked to watch their partners making love with other men, and the only reaction I had

(being naturally open to new experiences and seeing no moral obstacle) was to adapt willingly to their ways. But I have never drawn any theory from this, and I have therefore never been militant about it.

There were five of us, three boys and two girls, and we were finishing our lunch in a garden on a hill above Lyon. I had come to see a young man I'd met recently while staying in London, and I had taken advantage of the fact that a friend's boyfriend, André (who was from Lyon himself), was driving down from Paris. On the way, when I asked if we could stop so that I could have a quick pee, André came and watched me and stroked me as I squatted. It was not an unpleasant situation but it did make me feel slightly ashamed, and it was perhaps at that precise moment that I learned to sidestep my embarrassment by burying my head between his legs and taking his cock in my mouth. When we reached Lyon, I stayed with André and we went to stay with some friends of his, a boy called Ringo who lived with an older woman whose house it was. The latter was away, and the boys had made the most of this and organised a little party. Another boy came and brought a girl, a tall, lanky tomboy with very short, coarse hair.

It was in June or July, it was hot and somebody suggested that we should all take our clothes off and jump into the big pond. I heard André's voice saying his girlfriend wouldn't be bashful in coming forwards, and his words sounded a little muffled because I did indeed already have my T-shirt over my head. I forget when and why I stopped wearing underwear (even though as soon as I was thirteen or fourteen my mother had made me wear an underwired bra and a panty girdle on the pretext that

14

a woman 'should be held in place'). In any event, I was naked almost immediately. The other girl started getting undressed too, but in the end no one went in the water. The garden was exposed; and that is probably why the next set of images that come back to me are in a bedroom, me nestled in a tall, cast iron bed, all I can see through the metal bars are the brightly lit walls, aware of the other girl lying on a divan in one corner of the room. André fucked me first, quite slowly and calmly as was his manner. Then he stopped abruptly. I was overcome with an ineffable feeling of anxiety, just long enough to see him moving away, walking slowly, his back arched, towards the other girl. Ringo came and took his place on top of me, while the third boy, who was more reserved and spoke less than the other two, rested on one elbow beside us and ran his hand over my upper body. Ringo's body was very different from André's and I liked it better. He was taller, more wiry, and Ringo was one of those men who isolate the action of the pelvis from the rest of the body, who hammer without smothering, supporting their torso on their arms. But André seemed more mature to me (he was in fact older and had served in Algeria), his flesh was not so spare, he already had less hair, and I liked going to sleep cuddled up next to him with my buttocks against his belly, telling him we were a perfect fit. Ringo withdrew and the one who had been watching and stroking me took his turn even though I had been resisting a terrible urge to urinate for some time. I had to go. The shy boy was piqued. When I came back he was with the other girl. I no longer remember whether it was André or Ringo who took the precaution of telling me that the shy boy had only gone to 'finish off' with her.

I stayed in Lyon for about two weeks. My friends worked during the day and I spent my afternoons with the student I had met in London. When his parents were out, I lay down on his cabin bed and he would lie down on top of me, and I had to be careful not to knock my head against the shelves. I was still inexperienced but I regarded him as still more of a novice than myself from the way he furtively slid his still slightly limp cock into my vagina, and the way he so quickly slumped his face down onto my neck. He must have been sufficiently preoccupied with what a woman's reaction might and should be to ask me whether the sperm projecting onto the walls of the vagina produced a specific sensation of pleasure. I didn't know what to say. I didn't feel his penetration that distinctly, whereas I certainly can distinguish a viscous little puddle spreading inside me! 'Really, that's strange, no special feeling?' 'No, nothing at all.' He worried more than I did.

The little gang would come and wait for me late in the afternoon at the end of the road. They were happy and playful, and, spotting them one day, the student's father said with a cordial note in his voice that I must be a hell of a girl to have all these boys at my disposal. In fact, I had given up counting. I had completely forgotten my childhood investigation into the permitted number of husbands. I was not a 'collector', and I thought that the boys and girls that I saw at parties mauling and being mauled, and mouth-to-mouth kissing until their breath gave out with as many people as possible so that they could boast about it the next day, were somehow offensive. I was happy simply to discover that the delicious giddiness I felt at the ineffably soft touch of a

stranger's lips, or when a hand fitted itself over my pubis, could be experienced an indefinite number of times because the world was full of men predisposed to do just that. Nothing else really mattered. I had nearly lost my virginity earlier to a boy I had met who made quite an impression on me. He had a slightly drooping face, huge lips and very black hair. No arm or hand had ever covered so much of my body surface as when I lay trapped by the sweater he had pulled up over my head and the sides of my knickers that he held taut across my groin. That was the first time that I had felt myself to be in the grip of pleasure. The boy asked me, did I 'want more'. I had no idea what that might mean, because I couldn't see what 'more' I could possibly have. In fact, I brought the session to an end and, even though I continued this flirtation, meeting up with him regularly in the holidays, I never thought to take it further. Neither was I particularly taken with the idea of 'going out with' someone – or with several people. I fell in love twice and with both men any physical relationship immediately became impossible: the first one had just got married and, anyway, showed no interest in me at all, the second lived a long way away. I therefore had little desire to hook up with a boyfriend. The student was too bland, André was as good as engaged to my friend, and Ringo had a long-term partner. And in Paris I had the friend I had made love to first, Claude, and he seemed to be in love with a bourgeois girl who could utter such poetic sentences as 'touch my breasts, they're so soft this evening', without letting him go any further. This example had quickly, if rather confusingly, taught me that I could not be classed as a great seductress, and that my place in the world was therefore not so much amongst the

women, facing the men, but alongside the men. Put simply, there was nothing to stop me constantly renewing the experience of tasting a different saliva every time, and blindly feeling with my hand for a form that would always be unexpected, a surprise. Claude had a beautiful dick, it was straight and well-proportioned, and the memory I have of those very first couplings is a feeling of fullness, heaviness as though all of me had been stiffened and filled. When André unzipped in front of my face, I was amazed to find something smaller, and more malleable, because, unlike Claude, he was not circumcised. A dick which is constantly exposed demands to be looked at, it provokes sexual excitement with its smooth monolithic contours, whereas the foreskin that you can play back and forth, uncovering the glans like a great bubble forming on the surface of soapy water, elicits a more subtle sensuality, its suppleness bending in waves to the partner's orifice. Ringo's dick was more like Claude's, the shy boy's more like André's, the student's belonged to a category that I would recognise later, those which, although not necessarily larger, are covered in a thicker outer layer, making them feel immediately more substantial in the hand. I discovered that every kind of dick required different movement, different behaviour from me. And just as every time I had to adapt to another kind of skin, another complexion, different degrees of hairiness, different amounts of muscle tone (it goes without saying, for example, that not only do you hold on to the torso above you in a different way if it is smooth as a stone or filled out with the beginnings of a bosom or obscuring your view with a thatch of hair, but also that these images do not have the same resonance in your

18

imagination. As a result, with retrospect, I seem to have been more submissive with the clean cut or slightly rugged bodies that I perceived as truly male, whereas I took more initiative with heavier bodies that I feminised, however big they may have been), by the same token, the consti- tution of each body seemed to induce its own stances.

I have pleasant memories of a very wiry body with a slender shaft which rammed into my arse as I offered it up into the air, thrusting in a series of jerks, and as if from a distance without any other part of my body really being touched, apart from my hips held in his hands; conversely, I didn't like it – not that I ever tried to get away – when fatter men, to whom I was nevertheless attracted, covered me too fully and, matching their behaviour to their corpulence, they tended to give smoochy kisses and to lick my face. In short, I entered my adult sexual life in the same way that, as a child, I went into the tunnel on the ghost train, blindly and for the pleasure of being jostled about and grabbed as chance would have it. Or, you could say, swallowed up by it as a frog is by a snake.

A few days after I got back to Paris, André sent me a letter to warn me, tactfully, that we all had the clap. My mother was the one who opened the envelope. I was sent to the doctor and banned from going out. But from then on my own sense of propriety, which had become extremely intransigent, no longer tolerated the fact that I lived with my parents now that they could imagine me in the act of making love. I ran away from home, they brought me back; eventually, I left for good to go and live with Claude. The clap had been my baptism; after that, for many years, I lived in mortal terror of that scissoring pain even though it struck me as being nothing more than

a distinguishing sign, the shared fate of those who fuck a lot.

'Like a nut in its shell'

In the biggest orgies in which I participated, from that time on, there could be up to about 150 people (they did not all fuck, some had come to watch), and I would deal with the sex machines of around a quarter or a fifth of them in all the available ways: in my hands, my mouth, my cunt and my arse. Sometimes I would exchange kisses and caresses with women, but that was always less important. In the clubs, the proportion was far more variable depending, obviously, on the clientele but also on the customs of each place – I will come back to that. It would be much more difficult to make an estimate of the evenings spent in the Bois de Boulogne: should I count only the men that I sucked off with my head squashed next to their steering wheels, or those with whom I took the time to get undressed in the cabins of their trucks, and ignore the relay of faceless bodies behind the car doors, one hand manically rubbing up and down their cocks in diverse stages of erection, while the other hand dived into the open car window to energetically knead my breasts? Today, I can account for forty-nine men whose sexual organs have penetrated mine and to whom I can attribute a name or, at least, in a few cases, an identity. But I cannot put a number on those that blur into anonymity. In the situations I am describing here, and even if there were people I knew or recognised at an orgy, the confused succession of embraces and couplings was such that if I

could distinguish individual bodies, or at least their attributes, I could not always distinguish the people themselves. And even when I refer to the attributes, I have to admit that I did not always have access to all of them; some exchanges are very ephemeral and, if I recognised a woman by the softness of her lips, I would not necessarily recognise her touch which could be fiercely energetic. Sometimes, I would only realise after the fact that I had been fondling a transvestite. I was abandoned to a hydra. Until, that is, Éric broke away from the group to prize me out of it, in his own words, 'like a nut from its shell'.

I met Eric when I was twenty-one, not before his existence had been 'announced' to me; some mutual friends had frequently assured me that, given my pre-dispositions, he was just right for me. After the holiday in Lyon I had continued having group sex with Claude. With Éric, the regime intensified, not only because he took me to places where I could, as I have just shown, make myself available to an incalculable number of hands and penises, but more particularly because the sessions were well organised. To my way of thinking, there has always been a clear-cut difference between, on the one hand, the more or less improvised situations which lead a group of people to redistribute themselves amongst the beds and sofas after a dinner, or which induce an excited gang of friends to drive around the porte Dauphine in their car until they make contact with other cars and all the passengers end up intermingling in a large apartment, and, on the other hand, the soirées curated by Éric and his friends. I preferred the inflexible sequence of the latter, and their exclusive goal: there was no rush and no tension: there were no outside factors (alcohol, demonstrative

behaviour . . .) to impede the flow mechanics of bodies. Their comings and goings never strayed from their insect-like determination.

Victor's birthday parties impressed me the most. At the entrance to his property there were guards with dogs, talking into walkie-talkies, and I was intimidated by the crowds of people. Some women had dressed for the occasion, they wore transparent blouses or dresses, I was envious of them, and as people arrived and met up, sipping their champagne, I stood to one side. In fact, I only really relaxed once I had removed my dress or my trousers. My true clothing was my nudity, which shielded me.

I was amused by the architecture of the place because it was similar to the décor of a then very fashionable boutique on the boulevard Saint-Germain, called the 'Gaminerie'. It was, on a larger scale than the boutique, a cave, with its attendant cells, fashioned in white stucco. This 'grotto' was underground and its only source of light came from the bottom of a swimming pool on the floor above. Through a pane of glass which formed a sort of vast television screen, we could see the succession of bodies diving in from the upper floor. I am describing a place in which I have never moved through a great deal. The scale of things had changed around me, but my situation was not very different from what it had been the first time, with my friends in Lyon. Éric would settle me on a bed or a sofa in one of the alcoves, respecting some vague custom by taking the initiative to undress me and put me on display. He might start to rub me and to kiss me but then would immediately hand me over to others. I

would almost always stay on my back, perhaps because the other most common position, in which the woman actively straddles the man's pelvis, is less adapted to intervention from several participants and, anyway, implies a more personal relationship between the partners. On my back, I could be stroked by several men while one of them, rearing up to make room and see what he was doing, would get going in my vagina. I was tugged and nibbled in several places at once; one hand rubbing insistently round the available part of my pubis, another one skimming broadly across my entire torso or choosing to provoke my nipples ... More than the penetrations, I took pleasure in this caressing, and in particular when it was a penis that was trailed over the entire surface of my face or a glans that rubbed against my breasts. I liked to catch one in my mouth as it passed by, running my lips up and down it while another came and begged attention on the other side of my outstretched neck, before turning my head to take the newcomer. Or having one in my mouth and one in my hand. My body opened up more under the effects of this kind of stroking, which was relatively brief and could be renewed again and again, than in penetration itself. On that subject, what I remember most is the stiffness between my legs after being pinioned sometimes for four hours, especially as many men tend to keep the woman's thighs spread well apart, to make the most of the view and to penetrate further. When I was left to rest, I would become aware that my vagina was gorged. It was a pleasure feeling its walls stiffened, heavy, slightly painful, in their own way bearing the imprint of all the members that had touched base there.

The position of the active spider in the middle of her

web suited me well. Once – and this was not at Victor's house but in a sauna at the place Clichy – I hardly left the depths of a big armchair the whole evening, even though there was a huge bed in the middle of the room. With my head on a level with the dicks that made themselves available, I could suck at one while, with my hands on the arm rests, I jerked off two more at the same time. My legs were lifted up very high and, one after another, those who had become sufficiently aroused, followed through in my cunt.

I sweat very little but sometimes I was drenched in my partners' sweat. There would also be threads of sperm that dried along the tops of my thighs, sometimes on my breasts or my face, even in my hair, and men who are into orgies really like shooting their load in a cunt that's already lined with cum. From time to time, on the pretext of going to the toilet, I would manage to extricate myself from the group and go to wash. Victor's house had a bathroom with a bluish light which was clear enough without being violent. A mirror took up the entire wall above the bath, and the deep, hazy image it reflected softened the atmosphere still further. I saw my body in it, and was amazed to see that it was smaller, slimmer than it had felt a few moments earlier. In there, more gentle exchanges took place. There was always someone there to compliment me on my olive skin or on the *savoir faire* I demonstrated with my mouth – very different from when, buried under bodies, I could hear, as if from a long way away, a conversation about myself, rather like a sleeping patient making out the doctor's and the interns' comments as they made their rounds of the beds.

A jet of water on my open, replete pussy. But few were the times when a man who had also come there for a

pause did not make the most of the moment when I squatted over the bidet to jiggle his softened but always willing dick against my lips. And quite often, scarcely freshened up, I would stand and put my hands on the washbasin, offering my vulva to increasingly firm pressure from an organ that eventually managed to deliver a few thrusts. One of my favourite delights is the pleasure given by an organ that slips between the labia like that and then affirms itself there, progressively separating them, before burying itself in what I have had plenty of time to establish is an eagerly accommodating space.

I have never had to suffer any kind of clumsiness or brutality, and I have been lucky with the attentiveness of my partners. If I was tired or the position was becoming uncomfortable, I only had to let it be known, often using Éric as my intermediary because he was never far away, and I would be left to rest or to get up. In fact, the unforced kindness, almost amounting to indifference, which surrounded me at orgies perfectly suited me as I was then, young and awkward in my relationships with other people. The population in the Bois was more mixed – socially, too – and I think that there I probably sometimes came across men who were even more shy than myself. I saw little of their faces, but I would catch some of them looking at me with something approaching caution in their eyes, or even amazement. There were the regulars who knew the place well and would briefly take the initiative in organising the goings on, and there were the more furtive ones, and there were also those who watched, without joining in. Even though the venue and the participants changed from time to time, and Éric made it his job to find new permutations – with me always

following a little apprehensively – what paradoxically gave me pleasure was identifying familiar feelings in unusual circumstances.

One particular episode was full of contrasts. I had found a space on one of those concrete benches with a really rough, grainy surface. A group had formed: I had the groins of three or four men around my head, wanting me to take them in my mouth, but I could also catch glimpses of the pale hands of the outer circle as they traced their rhythmic action on their dicks in the darkness, like coiled springs quivering to the touch. Behind them there were a few more shadows looking on. Just as someone was beginning to lift up my clothes, we heard the graunching sound of a car crash. I was left alone. We were in one of those little clumps of trees planted along the boulevard de l'Amiral-Bruix near the porte Maillot. I waited a moment and then went and joined the group in the clearing between the hedges. A Mini had run straight into one of the bollards down the centre of the avenue. Someone said there was a young woman inside. A crazed little dog was running up and down. The bulb inside the bollard and the car headlights were still on, creating a strange blend of yellow and white light. We must have heard the sirens of the emergency services quite soon, because I went back to the bench. As if the space inside the little copse had been elastic, the circle formed again and the actors picked up the scene where it had been interrupted. A few words were exchanged; the sight of the accident suddenly reinforced what had been a tacit link between us, and there I was back with my ephemeral little community, completely at one with its focused and very unusual activity.

I liked slipping into the rare snatches of conversation and the more ordinary gestures and positions which, in the Bois, both tempered and highlighted the more extraordinary encounters. One evening when the porte Dauphine was virtually deserted, our car headlights picked out two very tall black men standing on the edge of the pavement. They looked as if they were lost or waiting, in this desolate backwater, for an improbable bus. They led us to a place nearby, to a little attic room. The room and the bed were both narrow. They took me one after the other. While one was on top of me, the other sat on the corner of the bed and made no attempt to join in. He just watched. They made big slow movements and had long cocks like I'd never seen before, not too thick and able to penetrate very far without my having to spread my legs too wide. They were like twins. Two gentle unhurried couplings in a row. They touched me with a sort of precision and in return I revelled in the vast skin surface that they presented to me. I really think that, that particular time, I took the time to feel each stroke of their patient penetration. While I was getting dressed they chatted to Éric about the Bois de Boulogne and about their work as cooks. As we left they thanked me with all the sincerity of polite hosts, and my memory of them is full of affection.

At Chez Aimé, relations between people were not so civil. 'Aimé' was a very popular swingers club to which people came from very far away, even from abroad. Years after it had closed, I still marvelled like an awestruck schoolgirl when Éric listed the famous people – the film stars, singers, sports personalities and businessmen – I might have met there without actually opening my eyes

enough to recognise them. During the time that we went there, a film which parodied some aspects of sexual liberation came out. One scene took place in a club which looked like Chez Aimé; it showed a group of men thronging round a table. There was a woman lying on the table, but all you could see were her legs, in high boots, jiggling comically over their heads. Because those sort of boots were in fashion at the time, and I wore them, and even tended to keep them on when I didn't have a stitch of clothing on because they were difficult to remove, and because I must have brandished them in the air like that more than once as I lay on a table, I had the vanity to think that it might well be my minimal attire and my waving in the air that had fired the director's imagination.

The pleasure that I felt as I succumbed to a long session at Chez Aimé with my buttocks parked on the edge of a big wooden table and the overhead light hanging down over my torso as if I were some sort of board game, is equalled only by my loathing for the journey there. It was a long way from Paris; you had to drive through the sinister darkness of the Bois de Fausses-Reposes at Ville d'Avray, and then you had to find the house at the bottom of a skimpy garden which looked like something from the suburbs of my childhood. Éric never gave me any warning of the evening's agenda because I think he drew some of his satisfaction from elaborating it with surprises; it was his own way of creating weird and wonderful situations. Anyway, I played along by asking no questions. Even so, when I gathered that we were heading there, I would worry not only at the thought of all the strangers who would soon be forcing me to wake up to where I was, but also in anticipation of the energy I would

have to expend. It was a feeling not unlike that one gets before giving a conference, when I know I will have to be completely focused on what I am saying while in the hands of my listeners. In fact, both the men met in those situations and the audiences plunged in darkness are faceless and, miraculously, in between the anxiety of anticipation and the weariness at the end, you are perfectly unaware of your own exhaustion.

You went in through the bar – I don't remember ever actually being taken in there (even though feeling my pussy against the moleskin of a barstool with my flattened buttocks lending themselves to furtive fondling belongs to my very oldest fantasies). I'm not sure I even paid much attention to what was going on around me, to the few women perched by the bar whose buttocks and thatches passers-by certainly did play with. My place was in one of the back rooms, lying – as I have said – on a table. The walls were bare, there was no seating, there was nothing in these rooms except for the rough-hewn tables and ceilings lights. So I could stay there two or three hours. Always the same configuration: hands running over my body, me grabbing at cocks, turning my head from left to right to suck, while other cocks rammed my belly. Twenty could take it in turns in an evening. That position, the woman on her back with her pubis on a level with the man's as he stands squarely on the ground, is one of the most comfortable I know. The vulva is well opened, the man in just the right place to thrust horizontally and strike deeply without stopping. It makes for vigorous and precise fucks. I was sometimes set upon so violently that I had to hold onto the ends of the table with both my hands and for a long time I bore the scar of a little gash above my coccyx,

where my spine had rubbed against the rough wood.

In the end Aimé closed. We went one last time; the place was deserted and Aimé himself, his bulk hovering behind the bar, was quietly getting at his wife. He had been summoned by the police. He was angry with her because she had persuaded us not to come back later.

That evening we ended up at Les Glycines, my first visit to a place that seemed enchanting. Claude, a friend called Henri and me made the most amicable trio. Henri lived in a tiny apartment on the rue de Chazel facing the pale rough-cast surface of a high garden wall which hid a large private house. Because it was on the way, Claude and I used to stop off with Henri on our way home from our Sunday visit to our parents. The three of us would fuck together, both boys inside me at once, one in my mouth the other up my arse or my cunt, under the playful auspices of one of Martin Barré's loveliest paintings; we called it 'Spaghetti' and it had been given to Henri by the artist himself. Afterwards we would look out of the window, watching the comings and goings at Les Glycines. Henri had heard that the club was used by film stars, and sometimes we would think we'd recognized someone. We were just kids, the best kind of gawpers, fascinated and amused by this secret activity which we didn't even try to imagine, and actually more excited by the sight of things completely inaccessible to us: the swanky cars dropping people off, the classy deportment of the silhouettes who stepped out of them. When I went through the porch a few years later, I knew instantly that I preferred Chez Aimé's spare style.

We went up a little gravel path blocked by a group of Japanese visitors who had actually been refused entry by

the air-hostess-like girl on the door. The latter asked to see my Social Security card. Not in regular employment, I did not possess one, and even on the occasions when I was able to produce a payslip I would still be in the wrong because, even today, whenever confronted by a woman taller than me I turn into an awkward child. We did go in, all the same. It was lit up like a dining room, there were a lot of people, lying naked on mattresses on the floor, and what unsettled me even more than the threat of the 'employment officer' was that people were telling jokes. A woman with very pale skin, no make-up and tousled hair which still had the vestiges of the same French pleat as the hostess, was making everyone roar with laughter because her little boy 'really wanted to come with her this evening'. I can see Éric, who was always very practical, working his way along the skirting board looking for a power point, because we had managed to arrange a swap with a couple and it would have been nicer to dim the lights. There were little waitresses navigating between the bodies, holding aloft trays of champagne in flutes; one of them caught her foot in the electric cable and switched the light back on. She even accompanied the act with a loud 'shit'. After that, I don't recall us waiting for me to extract even the scantiest bodily emission.

Apart from in the Bois – even there, as we've seen, even there! – you don't mix with people until you have greeted them first, until you have respected a transitional moment in which a few words are exchanged, where each person maintains just the time and space between themselves and the others to offer them a glass or hand them an ashtray. I always wanted to abolish this suspense, but there were some rituals that I tolerated better than others. Armand

used to make me laugh because, while everyone else was still at the chatting stage, he would strip completely naked, a few minutes ahead of all the others, and would fold his clothes as carefully as a butler. Or I would comply with what I thought was a stupid policy of one group who would not swing until they had dined, always in the same restaurant, like an old school reunion; and what made their evening was to 'de-knicker' or 'de-tight' one of the women in their party while the waiter was going round the table. On the other hand, I thought it was obscene to tell salacious stories at an orgy. Was it because I instinctively made a distinction between the playlets presented as a prelude to a play – the better to prepare you for it – and the play-acting which serves only to delay it? The acts performed in the one are never performed in the other where they really would be 'out of place'.

Even if I have kept some of the reflexes of a practising Catholic to this day (secretly making the sign of the cross if I'm afraid something is going to happen, feeling watched as soon as I know I have done something wrong or made a mistake . . .), I can no longer really pretend that I believe in God. It's quite possible that I lost this belief when I started having sexual relationships. Finding myself vacant, then, with no other mission to fulfil, I grew into a rather passive woman, having no goal other than those that other people set for me. I am more than dependable in my pursuit of these aims; if life went on for ever, I would pursue them for all eternity, given that I did not define them myself. It is in this spirit that I have never wavered in the job I was given (a long time ago now) publishing *Art Press*. I was involved in its creation, and I

have dedicated myself to the work sufficiently to have been to some extent identified with it, but I feel more like a driver who must stick to the rails than a guide who knows where the port is. I've fucked in the same way. As I was completely available, I sought no more ideals in love than I did in my professional life, I was seen as someone who had no taboos, someone exceptionally uninhibited, and I had no reason not to fill this role. My memories of orgies, of evenings spent at the Bois or with one of my lover-friends are interlinked like the rooms in a Japanese palace. You think you are in a closed room, until one of the partitions slides back, revealing a succession of other rooms, and if you step forward more partitions open and close, and if the rooms themselves are numerous, the ways of passing from one to the other are infinite.

But trips to swingers' clubs hold little place in these memories. Chez Aimé was a different story: it was the very cradle of fucking. And I have remembered the disappointment of Les Glycines because it was the exemplary realisation of a dream I had carried with me since adolescence. Perhaps it is because my memory is chiefly visual and I remember more, for example, of Cleopatra – a club opened by some former customers of Chez Aimé – its extravagant setting in the middle of a shopping centre in the 13th arrondissement – than its neat décor and the activities to which I abandoned myself there; when all is said and done quite banal. On the other hand, other places and other events are so vivid that I could almost file them by theme.

There would be the image of a lively queue of cars, led by our own. And, as we are going up the service road on the Avenue Foch, I have an urgent need to pee. Four or

five cars brake behind us. As I get out and run over the strip of grass to squat next to a tree, car doors start to open; a few people, misunderstanding my manoeuvre, come over towards me. Éric rushes over to intercede, the place is open and very well lit. I get back into the car and the cortège sets off again. The car park at the porte de Saint-Cloud: suddenly the attendant sees fifteen or so cars diving into the tunnel one after the other, then surfacing again, in exactly the same order, an hour later. During that hour, I am taken by about thirty men, first of all several of them hold me up against a wall, and then they lay me on the car bonnet. Sometimes the script is complicated by the fact that we have to shake off a few cars on the way. The drivers agree on a destination, a line of cars forms up, and is spotted by others who join it, but then the file is too long and it is wiser to limit the number of participants. One night we drove around for such a long time that it felt like the beginning of a journey. One driver knew of a place, and then he admitted that he was no longer sure of the way. Through the rear windscreen I could see the pairs of headlights behind us navigating left and right, disappearing and reappearing. There were several stops, and several discussions, and eventually – on the terraces of a sports stadium somewhere in Vélizy-Villacoublay – I had the pleasure of the patient pricks of those who had not got lost along the way.

Drifting could have been another theme. Cars trundle along, stop, set off again, brake abruptly like remote-control toys. Little ploy at the porte Dauphine: we eye each other up from one car to the next and the password seems to be 'do you have a place?' So some cars leave the circle and we start on a sort of chase to an unknown

34

address. Once, and it's true it was only once, the search goes on a bit too long and we end up doing something foolish. I am with a group of friends who don't know the Bois very well; there are six of us squashed into a Renault and we're getting ready to go home after driving round in circles. We spot two or three cars down one of the many roads, we park alongside them and I, the brave and boastful little soldier going ahead in the name of all the others waiting behind me, go and give a blow-job to the driver of the car behind us. As luck would have it, two policemen come and take up positions in front of me when I withdraw. They ask the man who is awkwardly buttoning himself up whether he paid me, and they take down everybody's name and address.

Even when a memory centres on bodily facts, it is less the sensations than the atmosphere that is evoked first. I could gather together a good many anecdotes concerning the use to which for many years I put my anus as frequently, if not more, than my vagina. In a beautiful apartment behind the Invalides, during a small-scale orgy, in a room on a mezzanine floor with a long bay window and floor-level lighting like you find on American film sets, I am taken in that orifice by a giant's joystick. Is it because the coffee table in the sitting room is a giant resin model of an open hand in which a woman could easily stretch herself out luxuriously that the place itself somehow feels disproportionate and unreal? I'm frightened of this great Cheshire cat's organ when I understand by which route he is planning to penetrate, but he manages it without forcing too much and I am amazed, and almost proud, that size represents no obstacle. Neither does number. Was it because I was ovulating or had a touch of

the clap that at another orgy, a much larger one this time, I chose to fuck only with my arse? I can see myself at the foot of a very narrow staircase, in the rue Quincampoix, hesitating before deciding to go up. Claude and I were given the address by chance. We didn't know anyone. The apartment was very dark with a low ceiling. I could hear men nearby putting the word about, whispering: 'She wants it up the arse', or warning someone heading the wrong way: 'No, she only takes it from behind.' That particular time it did at the end hurt. But I also had the personal satisfaction of having had no feelings of restraint.

Imaginings

Reading through the pages above, still older images have come back to me, and these images were fabricated. How I conceived them, way before having my first experience and a very long time before I shed my innocence, constitutes a seductively appealing mystery. What shreds of the real world – photographs in *Cinémonde*; veiled comments of my mother's like the time when we left a café in which there was a group of young people only one of whom was a girl, and her muttering that the girl must be sleeping with everyone; or the fact that my father came home late at night, funnily enough having just come from that café – did I pick up and thread together, and what instinctual material did I formulate so that the stories I told myself as I rubbed the lips of my vulva together so accurately prefigured my future sexual adventures? I even remember a criminal case: the arrest of a rather obscure,

ageing woman (she must have been something like a maid on a farm) who was accused of killing her lover. I have forgotten the details of the murder because what really struck me was that amongst her belongings they found notebooks which she had filled with memories and into which she pasted little relics – photographs, letters, locks of hair – connected with her lovers, who turned out to have been extraordinarily numerous. As a child I loved sticking bits of plants and flowers into my holiday book, and I had a tidy scrapbook with precious photographs of Anthony Perkins or Brigitte Bardot, so I admired the fact that she had managed to collate this treasure, these traces of the men she had known within a few simple note pads of paper, and a secret corner of my libido was even more disturbed by the fact that this woman was ugly, alone, wild and outcast.

There are major structural similarities between situations I have lived and those I have imagined, even though I have never actively chosen to reproduce the latter in my life, and the details of what I have lived have had little part in nourishing my imaginings. Perhaps I should just assume that the fantasies forged in my earliest youth predisposed me to widely diverse experiences. Having never felt ashamed of these fantasies, and having reworked and embellished them rather than trying to bury them, they offered no opposition to what was real but rather a sort of mesh through which real-life situations that other people might have found outrageous struck me as quite normal.

My brother and I were rarely taken to play in the square, but there was a little one that we would cross on our way

to school. Down one side of the square there was a long wall with three pretty lean-to shelters. They were made of brick and wood, painted green and surrounded by shrubs. One was used for gardening tools, the others housed the public toilets. There must have been groups of boys hanging about in the square. In any event, the very first narrative that accompanied my masturbating – and one that I used again and again for very many years – put me in a situation where I was dragged into one of these shelters by a boy. I saw him kissing me on the mouth and touching me all over as his friends came to join us. They all started fondling me. We always remained standing, and I spun round in the middle of the tightly-knit group.

Most Sunday mornings my parents would take it in turns to take us to the matinee performance at the local cinema, whatever they were showing, and barely understood love stories glimpsed in fleeting sequences in romances and in the trailers, fired my imagination. I fantasised that I was allowed to go to the cinema alone. There were lots of people queuing. Suddenly someone would squeeze my arse. And again, everyone else around me in the queue followed the example, and when I reached the ticket desk, the salesgirl could see that my skirt had been lifted up, and I would talk to her while someone rubbed themselves against my buttocks; I didn't have any knickers on. The excitement rose. My top would be off by the time I had crossed the foyer (because I had formulated an image of myself as an adult blessed with resplendent breasts, an image I still resort to to this day in my fantasies, whereas my breasts are actually average size). Sometimes the manager of the cinema would ask us, calmly but with some authority, to wait until we were in

the auditorium to get on with our dishevelled embraces. At first, I would wriggle about with one boy, squeezed up to him in the same seat. He was the rather taciturn head of the gang who, having heated me to fever pitch, would then turn away abruptly and kiss another girl, abandoning me to his men, and we would drop in a heap to the carpeted floor between the rows of seats. The narrative continues: perfectly respectable men could leave their seats and their suspicious wives to cross the auditorium in the dark and prostrate themselves on top of me. Sometimes I would have the lights going back on while this cavorting was going on; or I would go to the toilets and there would be a succession of comings and goings between there and the auditorium. I think sometimes I would have the police intervening. Another take: the manager of the cinema would ask me to come to his office, and would then call for all the boys too. Another version: I followed the group who had adopted me in the queue all the way to a stretch of wasteland. And there, behind a picket fence, they would strip me naked and paw me. It was a compact group, forming a circle around me, like a second strip of fencing screening me from view. One by one, the boys broke away from the circle to press themselves against me. In another version, I was nestled deep in a seat in a nightclub with a man on either side of me. While I busied myself with one of them and we kissed each other hungrily, the other stroked my body. Then I would turn around and kiss the second one, but the first would not let me go, or he would give up his place to a third man, and so on; I kept swinging from left to right. I'm not sure that when I first started succumbing to these fabulations I had ever done any petting or even kissed a

single boy on the mouth. I was a late starter. When I came out of school I would quite often meet up with a group of friends in the bedroom that I shared with my brother, but it was usually to have fights with them. At that sort of age, girls' bodies are more mature than boys'; I was quite well built and I would sometimes win.

If I am going back as far as my imaginary constructions during my childhood and adolescence, I should point out the disparity which initially existed between these constructions and my actual behaviour, especially, as I recall, at puberty. I had started reading a Hemingway novel (*The Sun Also Rises*, perhaps), and I was sufficiently disturbed by the description of one of the female characters, due to the fact that she was attributed several lovers, to stop reading the book. I never went back to it again. A conversation with my mother also gave me a shock. I don't remember how we got onto the subject, I can just see her laying the table in the kitchen as she confided in me that she had had seven lovers in her life. 'Seven,' she said, looking at me, 'it's not all that many', but there was a shy questioning in her eyes. I scowled. It was the first time I had heard anyone say out loud that a woman could know more than one man. She became a bit defensive. A long time later, when I looked back on that rare moment of intimacy, I regretted my attitude. What was seven compared to a score that was still open?

When I was better informed about what sexual acts might entail, I obviously integrated them into my imaginings, but coitus achieved did not preclude the possibility of passing from one partner to another. One of the most detailed scenarios which illustrates this point of view was

the following: I am the guest of a vulgar, fat man – pretending to be an uncle – at a business meal in a private salon in a restaurant. There are twenty or thirty men sitting down to eat, and my first contribution is to do the rounds, sucking each of them off under the table. I can picture their faces above me, surrendering saggily, as each of them successively, and briefly, logs out of the conversation. Then I get up onto the table and they amuse themselves finding interesting substitutes for me to take, cigars, sausages, and someone comes and eats a sausage from between my thighs. As the meal goes on, I am conscientiously fucked, some leading me off to a sofa, others taking me standing up, from behind, bent over the table, while the discussions go on. The maître d'hotel and the waiters take their chances. If my masturbating has not yet been ended by an orgasm, then the kitchen boys finish me off. Finding myself in a group of men getting on with their different jobs and stopping only to come and join me in a casual, off-hand way, is a recurring scenario. A subtle alteration turns the uncle into a stepfather, and the conference into men playing cards (or watching football), and they take turns in coming to fuck me on a sofa while the others get on with their hand (or gesticulate at the television screen).

All my life I have gone back over, tinkered with and developed these few imagined situations with the application of someone composing a fugue, and those that serve me today are more or less altered versions of these originals. I mentioned brief film sequences which gave rise to certain fantasies. When it came out, I saw only an extract of Éric Rohmer's *La Collectionneuse*, on television. In a holiday house, a man goes into a room and walks past a couple making love on the bed with perfect

indifference; he just catches the young woman's eye. As I have gone back to this sequence again and again, my own transposition has created this: a delivery man comes into my house, although – oddly – I didn't have to open the door for him, and he finds me in my bedroom (where the half light is very like that in the film) watching a pornographic video. Without a word, he comes and lies down on top of me, and is soon replaced by a second delivery man, then a third, both of whom behave just as naturally. The story sometimes continues: a friend is coming to pick me up and I have to get ready. I carry on fucking standing up, taking care not to smudge my make-up or rumple my clothes, with my skirt lifted up over my back. The friend then actually takes the trouble to ring on the door bell, and I go to let him in, waddling like a duck with one of the delivery men's dicks burrowed in my cunt from astern. The friend, turned on himself, quickly unzips. Etc.

Sexual fantasies are far too personal for them ever really to be shared. Still, I had a powerful imagination and this gave me a well from which I could draw when, later, I started meeting talkers. In my experience, most men make do with a few expressions and catch phrases; you're their 'little sucker in chief', you're 'good at chewing nuts' before entering the ranks of the 'little bitch who's not too ashamed to stay like that all night', and you will rarely be 'rammed right up to the hilt' or 'fucked good and deep' without the incident being announced out loud. You encourage them, admitting that you're just a 'spunk bag', and as they reassure you that you're going to be given a good 'stuffing', 'rogering' or 'seeing to', you gasp and say 'it's so big', 'it's so hard' and 'it's so good' until you

eventually 'swallow the fountain', like the cat that got the cream. But these are just accentuations, reiterations punctuated by the mantra of interjections, gruntings and all the inflexions of the usual cries. Because, paradoxically, these words need less reciprocation than caresses do, dirty words are always more stereotyped and perhaps some of their power derives from the very fact that they belong to the most immutable inheritance. So, in the end, even words – which should help to distinguish us from each other – serve to fuse us all together and to accelerate the annihilation of the senses that we are all trying to achieve in those moments.

It is quite another story to construct a complete running commentary throughout the act, given by two voices, in counterpoint to the physical exchange.

Another man immeasurably – and quite fantastically – widened my understanding of fornicatory communion. He started the conversation by saying that he was going to take me to a hotel, there was little point in specifying what sort. There would be men queuing up by the bed, all the way out to the corridor. How much did I think they would pay to offload in my cunt? I suggested: 'Fifty francs?' The correct sum was whispered quietly in my ear: 'That's far too much. No, they'll give twenty francs to fuck you from the front and thirty to give it to you up the arse. How much of it are you going to take?'

Knowing that I always under-estimate, I ask 'Twenty?' A hard thrust of his dick given as a warning shot: 'Is that all – thirty!' Another stab in my vagina:

'You'll take a hundred and you won't wash.'

'There'll be young boys who'll shoot their load almost before they get inside me.'

'They'll do it on your stomach and your tits too, you'll be covered in it.'

'Yes, and there'll be some who are very old and very dirty, they won't have washed for so long that they'll have scabs on their skin.'

'Yes, and how much would you take to let them piss on you?'

'Will some of them crap on me too?'

'Yes, and you'll lick their arses afterwards.'

'And will I refuse to at first? Will I fight?'

'Yes, and they'll smack you.'

'It's disgusting, but I'll clean out the folds of their arseholes with my tongue.'

'We'll get there in the evening and you'll stay there till the following morning.'

'But I'll get tired.'

'You will be able to sleep, they'll carry on fucking you. And we'll come back that evening, and the hotel manager will bring his dog, and there'll be someone who'll pay to see you doing it with the dog.'

'Will I have to suck it?'

'You'll see, it'll have a very red cock and it'll climb on top of you like on a bitch and stay stuck to you.'

Other times, the events would unroll in the workmen's shed on a building site and whole teams of workmen would file through, paying no more than five francs a go. As I have suggested, my body sometimes convulsed in response to these images, but not always; the real action and the fantasy scrolled in tandem and only came together sporadically. We spoke in measured tones with all the precision and attention to detail of two scrupulous witnesses helping each other reconstruct a past event.

When he came close to orgasm my partner became less talkative. I don't know whether he was concentrating on one of the images of our imaginary film. As for me, I would sometimes bring the scenario back to a more private situation. The shed on the building site would become a concierge's *loge* in a building undergoing repairs. In those cramped quarters, the bed is sometimes just hidden by a curtain. Only my stomach and legs were visible in front of it, and the workmen still kept coming in droves to service me without my seeing them or their seeing me under the gaze of the concierge who regulated the traffic.

Communities

There are two ways of envisaging a multitude, either as a crowd in which individual identities become confused, or as a chain where conversely what distinguishes them from each other is also what links them together, as one ally compensates for another's weaknesses, as a son resembles his father even though he rebels. The very first men I knew immediately made me an emissary of a network in which I couldn't hope to know all the members, the unwitting link in a family joined as in the bible.

I have already let it be understood that I was reticent in social relationships and I saw the sexual act as a refuge into which I willingly abandoned myself as a way of avoiding looks that embarrassed me and conversations for which I was ill prepared. There was, therefore, no question of my taking any initiative. I never flirted or tried to pull. On the other hand, I was completely available: at

all times and in all places, without hesitation or regret, by every one of my bodily orifices and with a totally clear conscience. If, as Proust's theory goes, I see my own personality in terms of the image that other people have made of it, then that is the dominant trait. 'You never said no, never refused anything. You didn't make a fuss.' 'You were far from inert, but you weren't demonstrative either.' 'You did things so naturally, you were neither reticent nor dirty, just a tad masochistic from time to time . . .' 'At an orgy, you were always the first, right out there . . .' 'I remember Robert would send a taxi for you as if there was some emergency, and you would go.' 'People thought of you as some sort of phenomenon; even with an incredible number of guys you would still be the same, right up to the end, at their mercy. You didn't act the little woman who wants to please her man, or as the ballbreaking bitch. You were a mate who happened to be a girl, a girl-friend.' And also this note that a friend put in his diary and which still gives me a glow of pride to quote it here: 'Catherine who deserves the highest praise for her calmness and availability in every situation.'

The first man that I knew introduced me to the second. Claude was friendly with a couple of colleagues some ten years older than us. The man was not very tall but he had the muscle tone of a sportsman, she had a magnificent Mongolian face, with short-cropped blond hair; she also had one of those stiff personalities with which intelligent women sometimes modulate their sexual freedom. It could be that Claude had had some sexual encounters with her before introducing me to him, before, that is, arranging for me to fuck him. We carried on a sort of

loosely arranged swap which continued even after Claude and I had rented a studio next to their apartment. I would go and meet up with the man at their apartment, while she would join Claude in ours. The partition wall was like a television remote-control: there was a different film on if you switched sides. There was only one occasion when this disjunction was not respected. It was while we were on holiday in a house they owned in Brittany. A cold, mellow afternoon light permeated the sitting room right into the corner where he was resting on a daybed. I was sitting at the foot of the bed, she was coming and going, Claude had gone off somewhere. He gave me that weak, almost submissive, look that some men have even when they are expressing the most imperious of orders, then drew me to him, held my chin and kissed me, and then pushed my head down towards his organ. I liked it better like that. Using me to harden him up while I lay curled in on myself rather than stretching up to his face for a long kiss. And I sucked him off well. Perhaps it was on that day that I realised I had a gift for it. I concentrated on coordinating the way I moved my hand and my lips; from the pressure of his hand on my head, I knew when I should speed up or slow down the rhythm. But it was definitely the facial expressions that I remember most clearly. When I occasionally looked beyond the immediate horizon of his zip to take a deep breath, I saw her expression – as gently vacuous as a statue's, and his almost disbelieving. I now feel that it was then that I first hazily grasped the fact that, if relationships with friends could spread and grow like a climbing plant, twisting and knotting together in perfect and reciprocal freedom, and that all you had to do was to let yourself go with the flow of its sap, then all the more

reason for me to decide on my own behaviour for myself, resolutely and solitarily. I like this paradoxical solitude.

The art world is made up of a multitude of communities or families, and their rallying points – at the time when I started working as a critic – were more places of work, galleries and the editorial offices of magazines, than cafés. Naturally these little networks were breeding-grounds for casual romances. As I lived right on Saint-Germain-des-Prés, which was where the modern art galleries all were at the time, there was not far to go between an exhibition and a little cuddle. I can see myself on the pavement of the rue Bonaparte with a new painter friend, a shy boy who never really looked up as a smile spread across his face or as he peered at you through his thick glasses. I don't remember how he led me to understand that he wanted me, probably very warily ('I'd like to make love to you, you know'), perhaps even without touching me. I probably didn't give much of a reply. What I remember was how resolute I was. I took him all the way to my room. He let himself be led, without realising that he too was urging me on, weighing me down with those subjugated but tentative eyes. My pleasure derives from the precise moment when I have made the decision and the other feels a bit taken aback. I have an intoxicating feeling of fulfilling a heroine's destiny. But the best thing to put him at his ease is the girl-who's-just-escaped-her-parents'-clutches speech, I explain daffily that 'I want everything'. He carries on encouraging me with his attentive eyes. Someone who once took the same route has since admitted that my room under the eaves reminded him of somewhere you rented by the hour, and that the rather

coarse fabric which served as a bed cover seemed like a tarpaulin which had been thrown over it to protect it from the activities that were about to take place!

A group visit to an exhibition organised by Germano Celant in a Genoa museum. Claude, Germano and the others are walking ahead, I spend a little longer in each gallery, accompanied by William who has contributed to the exhibition. Quick, furtive gestures, he lands his hand across my snatch, I grind the bulge in his trousers, always amazed to find it so hard, like something inert, not like part of a living body. He has a very distinctive laugh, which sounds as if his mouth is already engaged in a long, deep kiss. He's having fun teaching me English: 'cock, pussy'. Not long after that, he spends a few days in Paris. As he comes out of the Rhumerie, he licks my ear and whispers 'I want to make love with you' leaving a little pause between each of the words. In the corner next to a service door at the back of the post office which stands where the rue de Rennes meets the rue du Four, I mutter my own English contribution 'I want your cock in my pussy.' Explosive laughter, the same trip all the way to the studio in the rue Bonaparte. William, like Henri and like many others, would return several times. We fuck there as a twosome and with others. The pretext is often a girl picked up by one of the boys and who needs a bit of persuading that it's even more fun when there are more than two to share in the pleasure. It doesn't always work and when it doesn't I am given the job of reassuring her, consoling her. The boys disappear discreetly to have a cigarette on the landing. I don't actually speak, I cajole, give her a gentle hug; girls are more easily conned by another girl. Of course, they could just leave, but not one

of them ever did, not even the one who remained friends with Claude and admitted, twenty years later, it was because she was still a virgin that she had refused to comply that evening and burst into tears. Henri remembers another girl: I locked myself into the kitchen – which also served a bathroom – with her to clean her face because her tears had smudged her mascara. He maintains that from the communal toilets on the landing he could hear us moaning through the skylights. She probably wanted to thumb her nose at the boys and I, perversely, went along with her.

By a curious inversion of sensitivity, although I am relatively blind to a man's seductive manoeuvres – quite simply because I prefer them to be kept to a minimum, but I will come to that subject shortly – I am always well aware when a woman is attracted to me, not that I have ever expected a woman to give me any pleasure. Oh, I am not denying the devastating delight of touching smooth, rounded, delicate skin which most women's bodies offer and only a very few men's! But I have only joined in these embraces and their related fumblings so as not to break the rules of the game. In fact, men who only ever suggest this sort of threesome strike me as boring and unimaginative, and I would quickly tire of them. I do, however, love looking at women myself. I could make out an inventory of the wardrobes, guess the contents of the make-up bags, and even describe the physiques of the women I work with better than their own male partners could. Out in the streets, I follow them and watch them more tenderly than any man trying to pick them up; I associate a particular conformation of the buttocks with a certain style of knickers, a particular wiggle in a walk

with the height of a heel. But my excitement is limited to a visual satisfaction. Beyond that I feel only a communal sympathy for hard-working women, for the huge fraternity of women who have the same first name as me (one of the most common names in France after the Second World War) and for the valiant warriors of the sexual liberation. As one of them once told me (and she herself was a genuine and affectionate dyke but also a swinger), 'giving the same man head brought us together; we are both dickheads'.

There was an exception: at an improvised orgy where half the participants had brought along the other half who were novices. I found myself alone for a long time on the thick black carpet of the bathroom with a blonde who had curves everywhere: cheeks, neck, breasts and buttocks of course, even down to the ankles. I was struck by her majestic name, she was called Léone. Léone had taken a little persuading before going with the flow. Now she was completely naked, like a golden Buddha in his temple. I was a little lower than her because she was sitting on the step that ran all the way round the raised bath. How had we ended up in that confined space when it was a huge, comfortable apartment? Perhaps because she had been indecisive and because I, once again, had felt compelled to take on the role of attentive initiator? My whole face burrowed noisily in her fleshy vulva. I had never sucked on such a swollen extremity and it really did fill my mouth, as Marseillais say, like a giant apricot. I latched onto her labia like a leech, then I dropped the fruit and stretched my tongue so far I almost tore its root, the better to dive into the extraordinary softness of her opening, a softness which makes the smoothness of breasts and

51

shoulders pale into insignificance. She was not the wriggling sort, she let out short, little moans, as soft as everything else about her. They resonated with sincerity and they gave me a tremendous feeling of exultation. As I put myself to good use suckling the little raised knot of flesh, it was so good letting myself go as I listened to her raptures! When we had all got dressed again with the fun and confusion found in sports club changing rooms, Paul, who spoke with less tact than the others, turned to her and asked: 'So? That was good, wasn't it? Don't we think she was right to let herself be talked into it?' She lowered her eyes and put a lot of emphasis on the first word as she replied that one person had certainly made an impression on her. I thought: 'Please, God, let it be me!'

We had found a ready-made philosophy reading Bataille but, when Henri and I look back on that fevered period, I think he is right when he says that our copulatory obsession and our missionary zeal derived more from a youthful playfulness. The bed in that tiny apartment was positioned in an alcove, which reinforced the feeling of snuggling in a hiding place, and when four or five of us thrashed about on it together it only meant that supper had turned into a round of 'I'll show you mine if you'll show me yours': the diners had tickled each other's parts under the table with their bare feet, or perhaps someone had proudly raised up a finger covered in particularly clear and slightly smelly sauce. Henri would make a game of bringing along a girl he had met only half an hour earlier in some arcade, and it was an adventure for our whole little team to wander the streets at four o'clock in the morning, looking for some poor girl's apartment, bent

on disturbing her tidy bed. Half the time, the ploy failed. The girl would let herself be fingered, would let someone take off her bra or her tights, but would end the evening clamped to a chair explaining that she really couldn't but, yes, she was very happy to watch, that was fine by her, yes, she would wait till someone could drive her home. I've sometimes caught glimpses of people, men or women in fact, taking refuge on an incongruous upright chair or balancing their buttocks on the edge of the sofa, unable to take their eyes off the pale limbs flailing the air a few centimetres away, a few centimetres which put them in a whole different time frame. They don't take part so you cannot really say that they are fascinated. Lagging behind – or shooting ahead – they are the patient, studious viewers of an edifying documentary.

Our zeal was, of course, only skin deep because the little challenges we set were intended far more for ourselves than for those we tried to initiate. Henri and I once failed on the boulevard Beaumarchais in one of the big, bourgeois apartments where intellectuals lived with bare parquet floors and inadequate overhead lighting. The friend who welcomes us has a thick beard, permanently parted by his bland laugh; he is married to a modern woman. All the same, she balks and goes to bed. We play at transgression, and I seem to remember quivering and roaring with laughter between their streams of urine. No, no, Henri corrects me, he was the only one to piss on me. In any event, what is for sure is that we had taken the precaution of getting into the huge cast iron bath. Then the three of us did go and fuck around on the balcony.

One of my girl friends puts me up for some months. I sleep in a tiny, little, unfurnished attic room, sometimes

with the cats for company. When her boyfriend comes to see her, she leaves the door to her bedroom wide open and neither of them makes any attempt to contain their exclamations. It never occurs to me to join them. I don't get involved in other people's business and, anyway, snuggled in my narrow bed, I think of myself almost as their little girl. But with that stubbornness peculiar to children and animals, I make quite sure that they get involved with my business. Given that, to some extent, I share her life, there is no reason why my beautiful hostess shouldn't systematically take the same cocks between her thighs as I do. It works four or five times. She resolutely allows herself to be pinned to the bed, her legs waving in the air like butterfly wings. I really like it when she looks right at Jacques (whose dick is reverberating from the twang of elastic when he pulled off his knickers) and says loudly that he's 'hung like a horse'. Jacques with whom I was just getting together at the time. He now reminds me that I once had a tantrum and set about kicking him wildly when he was fucking her. I had forgotten that too. Although, of course, I remember how I myself would niggle at the jealousies that other people never admitted. I feel as if I'm in a film about the free and easy lives of the young bourgeoisie when I go early one morning – stopping at the boulangerie on the way – to wake Alexis, who lives in a cute duplex on the rue des Saints-Pères. I notice the coolness of my skin next to his warm pyjamas, just moist enough to be good. He likes making fun of my promiscuity and he says that, at least at this time of day, he can be sure of being the first person of the day to penetrate me. Well, no, he isn't actually! I spent the night with someone else, and we had a fuck before I left, I've

still got his cum in my pussy. I stifle my exuberant laughter in the pillow. I can tell that he's a little upset.

Claude told me to read *Histoire d'O* and there were three ways in which I identified with the heroine: I was always ready; my cunt certainly wasn't barred with a chain, but I was sodomised as often as I was taken from the front; and finally, I would have loved her reclusive life in a house isolated from the rest of the world. Instead, I was already very active in my professional life. But the convivial atmosphere of the artistic world, the facility with which – despite my fears – I formed connections with people, and the fact that these connections could so easily take a physical turn led me to believe that the space in which this sort of activity was carried out was a well regulated closed world. I have already used the word 'family' several times. Sometimes this metaphor has not been a metaphor. For a long time I kept the adolescent trait of exerting my sexual attraction within a family circle, when a boy or a girl goes out with a girl or boy and drops them to go out with their brother or sister, or a cousin. I even had dealings with two brothers along with their uncle. I was a friend of the uncle and he often brought along his two nephews scarcely younger than myself. Unlike the times when this same man would take me to meet friends of his, on these occasions there was no preamble or stage management. The uncle would get me going and the two brothers would give me a good shafting. I would relax afterwards listening to their man's talk about some DIY gadget or some new software.

I am still on friendly terms with a number of men that I first knew as regular sexual partners. In other cases, we have just lost touch. I remember most of these

acquaintances with genuine pleasure. When I worked with some of them I found that the enduring intimacy and tenderness facilitated our collaboration. (Only once did I get angry about a serious work matter.) What's more, I never remove a person from their own network of friends and relationships or from the activities they enjoy. I had met Alexis as part of a group of young critics and journalists who were trying to set up new artistic publications. I was fucking two other people on the same circuit, and in fact Alexis had asked me, rather tartly, whether I had set myself a schedule to be 'shagged by every young critic in France'. We worked in a 'school's out' sort of atmosphere and my two other colleague-lovers, unlike Alexis, were still a bit rough around the edges even though they were already married. They both had spotty faces and did not exactly take good care of themselves. I gave in to one of them because, having been lured to his apartment on the pretext of a translation that needed checking through (another one of those cramped little apartments on Saint-Germain-des-Près), he had complained that, seeing I was sleeping with everyone it would be churlish of me not to sleep with him. The other had played his cards more confidently. He had arranged to meet me at his publisher's office, and the receptionist had told him I had arrived, adding with the consideration typical of women in her profession that the young woman waiting for him in reception was not wearing a bra under her blouse. The sexual relationship with the first came to a pretty abrupt halt, but with the second it went on for several years. Later, they both became collaborators on *Art Press*, and stayed there a long time.

I have suggested that I came to meet Éric having got to

know his friends, and heard what they had to say about him. Amongst these friends was Robert whom I met while putting together a piece on art foundries. In the event, he took me to Le Creusot where he was having a monumental sculpture cast. We travelled back at night and, during the trip, Robert joined me in the back of the car and lay full length on top of me. I didn't turn a hair. It was a narrow car and I was sitting sideways in my seat with Robert's head resting on my abdomen, and my pelvis over the edge to facilitate his groping. From time to time I would put my head down and he would give me little kisses. Glancing in the rear view mirror, the driver commented that I didn't seem to be on top of things. In fact the situation left me as dumbfounded as the visits to the foundries with their gigantic ovens. I saw Robert almost daily for quite a long time and he introduced me to a lot of people. I could instinctively distinguish between those with whom the relationship could take a sexual turn and those with whom it could not. An instinct that Robert also had; as a way of putting some of them off, he had come up with the idea of warning them that, as an art critic, I was beginning to wield some power. It was Robert who told me about that myth of Parisian life, Madame Claude. I have fantasised a great deal about being a high-class prostitute although I knew I was neither tall or beautiful, which I had been told you needed to be, nor distinguished enough for the job. Robert used to joke about the combination of my sexual appetite and my professional curiosity; he would say that I would be able to write a piece about plumbing if I went out with a plumber. And he always maintained that, given my personality, the person I had to meet was Éric. But in the

end, I met the latter through a mutual friend of theirs, a very edgy boy, one of those men who pounds into you with mechanical power and regularity, and someone with whom I had spent exhausting nights. In the morning, as if that wasn't enough, he would take me to the huge studio he shared with his work partner, and there, languidly tired, I would let this other man come over and take me in a silent, almost serious way. One evening this friend invited me to go and have dinner with him and Éric. As we already know, Éric introduced me to more men than anyone else, friends, colleagues and strangers. For the sake of accuracy, I must add that, at the same time, he introduced me to a rigorous way of working to which I still adhere.

For obvious reasons, the pattern in which these relationships are emerging, and the way in which individual incidents and deeds are recalled, overlap with aesthetic groupings. A painter friend called Gilbert, with whom I am reminiscing on my early beginnings, remembers that I restricted myself to discreet fellatio when I went and joined him in the afternoons in the apartment he shared with his family. Penetration was reserved for when he came to see me. In fact, on the first of these visits, he didn't 'finish' very satisfactorily because at the last minute I had asked him to switch to my arse. Such was my primitive method of contraception, bolstered by the image I had of my body as an integral whole with no form of hierarchy in terms of either morals or pleasure, and each of its individual parts could, in so far as was possible, be substituted for any other. Now it was actually another painter of the same school who made a point of teaching me to put my cunt to better use. I had pitched up at his

studio early one morning for an interview, not knowing I was going to find a very good-looking and forthcoming man. I don't think I left until the following day. As is often the case in artists' studios, the bed was positioned under a glass roof or a window, as if there was a need to establish what was going on within a framework of light. My eyelids can still feel the powerful light flooding onto my upturned head and blinding me. I must have had the same reflex of slipping his dick into my anus, just like that. Afterwards, he talked to me. He told me extremely persuasively that one day I would meet a man who would know how to take me from the front and to bring me to orgasm that way, and that it would be better than the other. Gilbert can't believe it when I tell him that at the time I was also seeing yet another of his painter friends (the short-sighted one whose insistent gaze carried me) whom he thought had never cheated on his wife; on the other hand, he himself reminds me of a third man with whom I used to participate in foursomes, still in the little studio on the rue Bonaparte, and that this man used to talk about the boys having sex between themselves. I am convinced that that was just a fantasy.

When William became part of an artists' collective I found myself spending the night with John, one of the members of the group. I had already met him several times and we had even talked at conferences together. I found him very attractive; he gave speeches about theory which my approximative understanding of English turned lurid, and as he talked the movements of his lips accentuated his fine cheekbones. I had come to New York to meet Sol LeWitt who had just started doing his pieces of torn and crumpled paper. When I arrived, I rang William to ask

him to put me up. I can see us now, standing in the loft he had just moved into, devouring each other with kisses, and him encouraging John to do the same. The walls only went three quarters of the way up to the ceiling and were arranged at right angles to each other to form rooms that seemed to be laid out in random cubes like a child's bricks. Four or five people came and went, apparently absorbed in some private task. William picked me up and carried me over to a mattress behind one of the walls. John was very gentle, providing a great contrast to William's nervous, abrupt movements. William left us and eventually John went to sleep. We had curled up together with his hand clamped onto my pubis. Early the following morning I had to extricate myself from his vice-like grip with the slow deliberate manoeuvres of a contortionist and to crawl out of the sheets onto the floor because, despite the light that was pouring in through the skylights, he was still asleep, and I ran into the street, caught a taxi to the airport and only just caught my flight. Even though I continued to follow that group's work, I didn't see John again for many years. When I did, during a retrospective, we exchanged but a few words because I found it so difficult to understand what he was saying.

As time went by, the shyness that I experienced in company was replaced by boredom. Even amongst friends whose company I enjoy, even if at first I follow the conversation and I am no longer afraid to join in, there always comes a moment when I suddenly lose interest. It's a question of time: all of a sudden I have had enough; whatever subject we are tackling I feel as if I'm turning to stone like when I watch one of those TV soaps which

recreates humdrum domesticity too accurately. It is irreversible. In these instances, tacit gestures – sometimes unseen ones – provide some escape. Even though I am not very enterprising, I have often improvised a little pressure from my thigh or a little crossing of ankles with the man next to me at the table, or – better still – the woman (it is less likely to have consequences) in the hopes of feeling that I am really a distant observer of this earnest assembly, busying myself with something else somewhere else. In the context of a communal life, on holiday for example, when a group of people do all sorts of things together, I have often felt the need to absent myself from outings and meals by doing this, acting randomly when the need arose. There were some particularly frenetic summers, defined by the incessant traffic between sexual partners, sporadically united in little orgies under the sun behind the low wall of a garden that overlooked the sea, or at night in the comings and goings between the many bedrooms of a villa. One evening I decide not to join in the fun, and Paul, who knows me well, gently makes fun of my decision; Paul – who sometimes forcibly holds me back, locking both of us into the bathroom if necessary, just to excite my impatience to mingle in the mêlée of bodies – promises to send me a friend of his that I have not yet met; someone who has nothing to do with the art world, a car mechanic. He knows that I would rather meet him than go to the restaurant with the others and sit wearily on a terrace or in the corner of a nightclub waiting for the same weariness to overcome the rest of them. I don't pay much attention to his proposition and I look forward to an evening alone. There is something delicious about those moments when the emptiness around you

opens up not only the space around you but also, some-how, the enormity of the time ahead. With unconscious economy, we make the most of this given opportunity by lazily settling into the very depths of an armchair as if to leave as much space as possible to the onrushing time. The kitchen is right at the back of the villa, and I go and make myself a sandwich. My mouth is full when Paul's friend appears in the doorway that leads out to the garden. He is tall and dark with pale eyes, quite impressive in the dark-ness. He apologises amicably, he can see that I'm eating, begs me not to stop just because of him . . . I am ashamed of the crumbs in the corners of my mouth. I say no, no, I'm not really hungry, and I chuck the sandwich away furtively. He takes me away. He drives his convertible along the Grande Corniche above Nice. He takes one hand off the steering wheel to reply to mine rubbing against the rough surface of bulge in his jeans. That swelling impeded by the tight, stiff fabric is an efficient stimulant for me every time. Do I want to go and eat somewhere? No. I think he's driving a bit further than he needs to, taking detours before getting home. He keeps his eyes on the road as I undo his belt. I recognise that little forward movement of the hips that a driver has to make to make it easier to undo the zip. Then there is the laborious process of extricating the member which has grown too big to slip straight out of the double envelope of cotton. You yourself have to have a wide enough hand to gather up all the parts in one smooth gesture. I am always afraid of hurting. He has to help me. At last I can get on with my conscientious hand job. I never start too quickly, I really prefer following all its length, feeling the elasticity of the fine sheath of flesh. I put my mouth to it.

I try to hold my body as far aside as possible so as not to be in his way when he changes gear. I keep to a moderate rhythm. I am conscious of the danger that driving in these conditions could represent, and, as a result, have no inclination to court it. As far as I can remember, it was a very pleasant encounter. Even so, I didn't want to stay the night with him and he had to take me back to the villa before the gang got back. It is not that I had forbidden myself sleeping out, but that I wanted the time I had spent with him to stay as it was (like when your thoughts wander off into a daydream half way through a conversation), a private place to which the others, for once, would not have access.

The reader will have realised that, as I have explained above, I exercised complete free will in my chosen sexual life and if, as I have just illustrated, I orchestrated little breakaways, this latitude could only be measured in terms of its direct opposite: the way fate brings people together, the determinism of the chain in which one link – one man – links you to another, which links you to a third and so on. Mine was not the kind of freedom played out on the whims of circumstances, it was a freedom expressed once and for all, an acceptance to abandon oneself unreservedly to a way of life (like a nun saying her vows!) I have never formed a relationship – however fleeting – with someone I have met on a train or in the metro, even though I have frequently heard stories of feverishly erotic encounters in such places, not to mention in lifts or restaurant toilets. I have always cut them short, rather abruptly even. I discourage them, humorously and gently, I hope, but in such an offhand way that it must look like

firm resolution. Engaging myself in the playful meanderings of seduction and, however briefly, keeping up the teasing banter which necessarily occupies the interval between a chance meeting with someone and accomplishing the sexual act with them, would be beyond me. At a push, if it were possible for the thronging crowds at a station or the organised hordes in the metro to accept the crudest accesses of pleasure in their midst as they accept displays of the most abject misery, I could easily undertake that sort of coupling, like an animal. Neither do I belong to the category of women who are 'looking for adventure' and I have been successfully chatted up only very rarely, and, even then, never by strangers. On the other hand, I have willingly accepted to go on dates arranged on the telephone by a voice purporting to have met me at some function or another, but to which I could not put a face. I was easy to find; they just had to call the magazine. That was how I ended up at the opera one night, at a performance of *La Bohème* . . . I arrived late and had to wait till the end of the first scene before I could go and sit down in the darkness next to my quasi-stranger. We had met, if you could call it that, a few days earlier at a mutual friend's party (when the relationship returns to the realms of a possible one-on-one, men rarely use the term 'orgy'), but the profile I could see, the balding head and the jowly face didn't mean a thing to me. I suspected that he had indeed been at the party but had not approached me there. He risked putting a hand on my thigh, looking at me furtively with something approaching anxiety in his eyes. He never shook off his air of weariness; he had a habit of rubbing his head in the same way that he ran his great bony hands over me, doing

64

it mechanically and complaining of terrible headaches. I thought he had a screw loose and there was something rather pitiful about him. I saw him again several times; he took me to shows and to very expensive restaurants which I found more than a little entertaining, not because I could be mistaken for a prostitute but because I could outwit the usherettes, the waitresses and the bourgeois clients around us, given that it was with a bona fide intellectual that the bald gentleman with the drooping skin was in conversation.

To this day, Hortense (the switchboard operator at *Art Press*) sometimes puts through someone whose name I don't recognise. 'They won't take no for an answer, they say they know you well.' I take the call. From their carefully chosen words spoken in conspiratorial tones, I quickly realise that the stranger thinks he is talking to a particularly good-time girl, the sort, if I'm not mistaken, who leaves a man with some very good memories. (Similarly, if I am introduced to someone at a private view or a dinner, and I feel that I am meeting them for the first time but that he delves his eyes into mine for rather longer than is necessary, saying 'but we've already met', I tend to think that, in what feels like another life for me, he had an opportunity to look at my face at leisure while my gaze may have been locked onto his pubic hair.) I may no longer have the curiosity to take it any further, but I still have a profound admiration and sympathy for the suspension in time in which swingers live.

It could be ten years, not to say twenty or more, since a man has had the pleasure of a woman, he still talks about it and addresses her as if it were yesterday. Their pleasure is like a hardy perennial which knows no seasons. It

flourishes in a greenhouse, isolated from outside contingencies so that they always see the body they held in the same way, even if it is now withered or lying stiffly in a robe. Be that as it may, experience has taught me that they cannot deny the principle of reality when it hits them in the face. As I don't warm to the telephone conversation, they inevitably ask a question, like a password which may or may not open the door. For example: 'Are you married now?' 'Yes.' 'Lovely, well, I'll give you a call next time I'm in Paris and perhaps we'll have a chance to see each other.' I know I will never hear from them again.

To go back to those preliminaries which many women claim to be the most delicious phase of a relationship, and which I have always tried to keep as short as possible, I should make it clear that I have only ever experienced them – and even then, without prolonging them – in two specific situations: when desire was already and unwittingly a breakaway faction of a profound and loving relationship, and after a relatively long period of abstinence: which amounts to exceptional circumstances.

In the latter case the signs were: an unexpected and frustrating sitting for a photographic portrait because – needless to say – the lighting was never quite right; a ride up in a lift which was about as chatty as a funeral vigil; tiny, furtive kisses, then sketchy little bites sneaked along the top of my naked arm when I had to place it on top of the lay-out table . . . I inhaled these libidinous emanations rather like an asthmatic who unwisely strays into a stifling hot-house. Very aware that I had done nothing to cultivate this sort of feeling in the past, I put them down to a sort of gentrification of my erotic life.

The other case proves that the sharpest of our sensual experiences can forge a path for itself even through our least sensitive points of access. Even though I have no ear at all, and I only ever go to the opera for reasons that have nothing to do with the art of music, it is thanks to his voice that Jacques first appeared on the horizons of the vast plain of my desire. And yet his does not correspond to the stereotype of a sexy voice, it is neither velvet nor cracked. Someone had recorded him reading a text and then played the tape to me over the telephone. I can still feel the echo it set up within me, radiating out to the most highly receptive point on my body. I gave myself up entirely to this voice which itself seemed to give up entirely every detail of its speaker, a voice with the clarity and the calm rhythm of its brief inflexions, as firm and assured as a hand turning up its palm to mean 'there you have it'. Some time later I heard it on the telephone again, live this time, pointing out a typo in a catalogue in which Jacques had been involved and on which I was working. Jacques offered to come and help me correct the copies. We spent hours on the work, just inches away from each other in a tiny office, with me very embarrassed by my mistake while he just got on with correcting it. He was attentive without being especially friendly. After one of these tedious sessions, he asked whether I would like to join him for dinner at the home of a close friend of his. After dinner, when several of us were squeezed next to each other on a bed serving as a sofa (which meant adopting an uncomfortable, semi-prone position), he stroked my wrist with the back of his index finger. It was an un-expected, unusual and quite delicious gesture, and it still moves me now, even when it is addressed to someone

else's skin. I followed Jacques to the studio he was living in at the time. In the morning he asked me who I was sleeping with. 'With lots of people,' I replied. 'Damn,' he said, 'I'm beginning to fall in love with a girl who's sleeping with lots of people.'

The Pleasure of Telling

I have never tried to hide the extent or the eclectic variety of my sexual contacts, other than from my parents. (As a child when a 'wedding night' was just a vague formula, even imagining that my mother would be able to picture me when that first night happened to me was truly a source of torment.) I have gradually and obscurely come to understand what this lifestyle had to offer me: the illusion of opening myself to innumerable possibilities. Given that, in other ways, I obviously had to comply with all sorts of constraints (a very demanding and stressful job, a destiny determined by poverty and, the worst shackle of all, the baggage of family conflicts and rows in relationships), the certainty that I could have sexual relations in any situation with any willing party (as a matter of principle, the illusion only held on condition that anyone unwilling was excluded from the horizon), was the lungfuls of fresh air you inhale as you walk to the end of a narrow pier. And, as reality did still impose limits on this freedom (I couldn't do just that, and even if I could, my thighs would have formed a link around only a tiny part of the human chain), this meant that the spoken word, the briefest evocation of episodes in my sexual life, should always conjure up the panorama of possibilities in

all their fullness. 'I am here, with you, but if I talk about it, I pull aside the sheet, I open up a breach in the wall, and I let in the entire army of lovers which surrounds us.' Usually, after about the third or fourth date, I would drop in a few men's names, connecting them with day to day activities which were, nonetheless, open to ambiguous interpretation, and – if I was feeling more confident – I would refer to a few picturesque situations in which I had made love in the past. I would evaluate the reaction. I have said that I did not go in for preaching, and even less for provocation, except as part of a well-meaning and harmless perversion, addressed only to people who had already been identified as kindred spirits. I was careful to be sincere, adhering to a dialectic with three terms: to some extent I protected myself from new relationships by branching out only if there was a connection with my community of swingers; that way I could identify whether or not the newcomer belonged to this community; finally, whatever his reaction, while still careful to protect myself, I would appeal to his curiosity.

As was quite right and proper, the friend who made me speak so much while we were fornicating insisted that, as well as evoking fantasies, I should talk about things that had really happened. I had to give names, describe places and say exactly how many times. If I failed to specify when describing a new acquaintance, he was quick to ask: 'Did you sleep with him?' But his interest did not focus exclusively on an obscene inventory ('What colour was his glans when you drew back his foreskin? Brown? Red? Did you give him one up the arse? With your tongue? or your fingers? How many fingers did you stick up his arse?'), it also extended to the more banal aspects of the setting:

'We were visiting an apartment to let in the rue Beaubourg, the carpet had balls of fluff all over it and he took me there and then on a mattress on the floor.' 'He's a bouncer for the Johnny Halliday show; that's how I saw the whole show from the side of the stage, it felt as if the speakers were inside me. We came home on his Harley Davidson; it didn't have any back seat left and the frame was carving into my pussy; when we did eventually fuck I was already spliced open like a ripe grapefruit.' An elementary form of sentimentality was always welcome: 'Was he in love with you?' me – 'hmm.' him – 'I'm sure he's in love with you.' me – 'The other morning I was pretending to sleep and I heard him whispering "I love you, Catherine; I love you, Catherine," and these breathy words were accompanied by a little movement of his belly, not as if he were fucking but more like a big cat twitching in its sleep.' A sentimentality corrupted by the jealousy of a third party: 'Does he know you fuck the whole gang? He's jealous isn't he?' The antics of another friend of mine who fucked me by lying me down on his work table right in the middle of a high tech studio, while presenting his dick like a monstrous pistil emerging from the corolla of floaty, crotchless women's knickers – a baroque touch in that austere setting – particularly appealed to him. I had to narrate it dozens of times, without having to embellish it with variations and even after I had stopped seeing the other friend. If I could come shortly after masturbating, that morning when I woke up, or in the office, in such and such a position and having made myself come x number of times in succession, that was good too. I never invented an adventure that hadn't happened, and my descriptions betrayed reality no more than any transposition inevitably

does. As I have already pointed out, the realm of fantasy and the realm of experience may well be close neighbours but, to me, they are still independent of each other like a landscape painting and the corner of the countryside that it actually represents; there is more of the artist's interior vision than reality in the painting. The fact that, from then on, we see that reality through the prism of the painting does not stop the trees from growing or their leaves from dropping. It is not unusual, at an orgy, for a man occupying a pussy that has already been well reconnoitred to worry about the effect his predecessors may have had. 'You were crying out earlier. Tell me about it. He's got a big cock, hasn't he? He must have really had to ram it in and you liked it. You were behaving like a woman in love. Don't deny it, I saw you.' I have to admit that sometimes, contrary to expectations, I would reply honestly – no, I liked his cock just as much – because at the time I hadn't learned to correct my scrupulous instincts, but also because of my writer's unwillingness to repeat myself.

But usually this chronicling of events took place outside of carnal exchanges. In that instance, the words hang in the space between those who are speaking, like a house of cards built up by their play of questions and answers, and which they hope won't suddenly crumble in the face of prematurely salacious confessions or a curiosity which too quickly becomes indiscreet. While driving in his clapped out little car, one friend asked me almost curtly: How old were you when you started to swing? What sort of people did you meet at orgies? Middle class types? Were there lots of girls? How many men had you in one evening? Did you come every time? My replies were equally matter of fact. At one point he pulled in by the side of the kerb, not

so that we could touch each other but to pursue the interrogation, his face quite relaxed, his eyes focused well beyond the end of the street. Did I take several at the same time, in my pussy and in my mouth? 'That's tops, and giving two others hand jobs at the same time.' This particular friend was a journalist; he ended up interviewing me for a review he wrote for.

In my immediate circle of friends, it was a question of keeping the excitement at a certain level verbally so that all the members of the club could clandestinely identify each other anywhere, at a work-related meeting or at a party, and could tolerate the potentially conventional nature of the event, for example at a house-warming party where there are lots of guests. They come and go in the huge studio where there isn't anywhere to sit. 'Is that guy there the one you have such a fantastic time with? That's great; he's not much to look at, but that doesn't mean anything. What the hell does he do to you?' I reply with a nod of the head; it's true that he's ugly and, more than that, he's out of place here. In my wanderings I come across lots of different kinds of people and I like arranging for these worlds to meet. I made sure he was invited even though they didn't know him. Someone comes and asks me who the guy is in the hopelessly outdated hippie smock. All the same . . . When I spend the night with him, lying on top of each other on his bed, we suck each other off for hours. During a sixty-nine it really gets me going to rub my breasts against a slightly rubbery tummy. 'It's true, you seem to go for chubby ones.' me – 'I dreamt I met François Mittérand at an orgy! . . . and I like them not that clean too . . . I'm pretty sure he never brushes his teeth.' 'You're disgusting. He's married isn't he?' me – 'I've seen a picture

of his wife. So ugly you wouldn't believe it . . .' That gets me going too. My voice is no louder than usual, but I give details only sparingly. I take pleasure in evoking this dirtiness and this contagious ugliness, at the same time savouring the disgust of the man questioning me. 'You suck each other. And then?' me – 'You can't imagine the way he moans . . . when I lick his arse . . . he gets in the doggie position, his arse is so white . . . he wriggles it when I burrow my nose into it. Then I get onto all fours . . . He finishes quickly, with short little thrusts which are – how shall I put this – very precise.' The man I'm talking to swings too but I happen never to have slept with him. I'm not especially attracted to him either. The man I'm referring to is not the sort to assail me with questions but he listens to me and, in the end, because everyone ends up calling their friends' friends by their first names even if they haven't met them themselves, I think of him as part of the group.

The more sociable I became, the better I cultivated my innate pragmatism in all aspects of sexual exchanges. Having, in the early days, tested various partners' receptivity to triangular games, I adapted the words I used. A faint, luxurious aura around me was enough for some whereas others, as I have illustrated, wanted to enjoy by proxy every last fingering. Added to this is the fact that even the most truthful speech is obviously never absolute, is always indexed by the way feelings have evolved. I was very talkative with Jacques at first but then I had to cope, more or less well and anyway belatedly, with the ban imposed on sexual adventures and accounts of these adventures the moment our relationship was perceived and lived as one of love, even though more than

once I read descriptions of erotic scenes in Jacques' books which could only have been reworkings of anecdotes I had told him. Of all the men that I saw for any length of time, only two brought my panoramic exposés to an abrupt halt. And even then I am pretty sure that these details they didn't want to know, and which were therefore not mentioned, still formed a central part of our exchanges.

Those who obey moral principles are probably better equipped to confront demonstrations of jealousy than those with a libertine philosophy which leaves them feeling helpless in the face of passion. A person can prove their extensive and sincere liberality by sharing the pleasure they take with the person they most love, only for it to be pierced, without any warning, by an exactly proportional intolerance. Jealousy may have been bubbling within them like a source, and as the bubbles burst they might even have been giving a regular and subterranean form of irrigation to their libidinal field, until – suddenly – they formed a torrent and then the entire conscious mind is submerged by it, as has been described by so many people. I have learned this from observation as well as from experience. I personally have experienced my confrontations with these passionate expressions of jealousy in a sort of daze which even the brutal death of a loved one did not provoke. And I had to read Victor Hugo, yes, I had to go and seek out that portrayal of God the father, to understand that this torpor is comparable to the sort of denial displayed by children. 'To accept facts as they are does not belong to realms of childhood. [A child forms] impressions as his terror grows but without making any connection between the two and

without drawing any conclusions,' I once read in *L'Homme qui rit*, finally finding an explanation for my mindless inertia. And I can confirm that, even after you have done all the growing you should do, you can still experience what I would describe as follows: a misunderstanding of an injustice which even stops you from seeing the feelings within that injustice. I was once beaten all the way along the path that runs from the rue Las Cases towards the area around the church of Notre-Dame-des-Champs, beaten and trampled in the gutter and, when I got back to my feet, forced to walk on by a series of punches to the top of my neck and my shoulders, the way they used to drive common thieves to the dungeons. We had just left a party which had had nothing of an orgy about it, but had at one point been enlivened by a sort of conga round the apartment during which a fairly prominent man had taken advantage of our passage through the ill-lit sitting room to push me onto a sofa and drench my ear with his saliva. And yet the friend who beat me had already come with me to other parties with much more dissolute ends. When, later that night, I retraced our steps all the way up the path, in the vain hope of finding a piece of jewellery which had fallen off under his blows, my thoughts were focused exclusively on this specific loss. On another occasion, one of my unwisely detailed accounts earned me a less furious – although equally aggressive – revenge: a slash with a razor on my right shoulder while I lay sleeping on my tummy, but not before the blade had been carefully disinfected on the gas hob in the kitchen. The scar that I still have, in the shape of a stupid little mouth, is a good illustration of what I felt at the time.

My own jealousy has been episodic. If I have used my sexual itinerary to satisfy my intellectual and professional curiosity, I have nevertheless remained perfectly indifferent to my friends' love lives and marriages. It even goes beyond indifference, perhaps contempt. I have had rushes of jealousy only with the men I have lived with and then, oddly, on a quite different basis in both cases. It pained me every time Claude was seduced by a woman whom I judged to be prettier than myself. I am not ugly, but on condition that you take my appearance as a whole, not thanks to anything remarkable about my features. It galled me that I couldn't enhance my sexual performances which, in principle, had no limitations – with a physical appearance which, itself, could not be improved. I would really have loved it if the girl who gave the best blow-job, the one who was always first to get going at an orgy, hadn't been short, her eyes slightly too close together, a long nose etc. I could describe incredibly accurately the physical traits that attracted Claude: a triangular face and the hairstyle of one of the secretaries whose slender chest provided a contrast to set off her rounded shoulders and conical breasts; the pale-coloured eyes of another woman, who had brown hair like myself; the smooth temples and doll-like cheeks of a third. It goes without saying that such a powerful contradiction to the principles of sexual freedom meant that this agony could not be articulated and, therefore, reduced me to scenes and crying fits that were all the more implacable, and hysterical displays worthy of a Paul Richer drawing.

With Jacques, my jealousy took the form of a terrible feeling of eviction. The images I could draw up of some woman who, in my absence, would hide the end of his

organ from view with her croup in a setting that was familiar to us, or whose whole enormous, ever expanding body inhabited the smallest part of our environment – the running board of the car, the leafy design of a sofa cover, the side of the sink you lean on with your tummy when you rinse out a cup – or whose hairs might even be left inside my motorbike helmet, these images caused me such acute pain that I had to extricate myself from them with the most drastic fantasising. I would imagine that, having caught them in the act, I would leave the house, set off along the boulevard Diderot towards the Seine, which wasn't far away, and throw myself in. Or I would go on walking to the point of exhaustion, and I would be taken to hospital, speechless and out of my wits. Another, less pathetic, escape route consisted in intensive masturbatory activity. As I have already begun to disclose the sort of narratives that sustain this activity, it might be interesting if I said something about the modifications they undergo at a given point. My wanderings over waste land and the delivery boy characters, profiteering phlegmatically from the situation, were replaced by a limited repertoire of scenes in which I myself no longer appeared and in which Jacques was the only male figure, accompanied by one or other of his girlfriends. The scenes would be partly imaginary, partly constructed from snippets harvested by trespassing into Jacques' notebooks or his letters, because he himself is not very talkative on the subject. Cramped in an Austin parked under a railway bridge, he keeps her head down on his belly, holding it carefully with both hands as if manipulating the glass dome that houses a precious object, until his cum has spurted into the back of her throat and he has heard the 'hic' as she swallows

reticently. Or a big white backside exposed on the sofa in the sitting room like a gigantic mushroom, and Jacques sinking into it as he slaps it smartly. Another option is for the girl to be standing with one foot up on a stool, in the position some women adopt to insert a tampon; Jacques, hanging on to her hips and braced on his tiptoes, pokes her in the same configuration: from behind. I would systematically orgasm at the point in my narrative when I allowed Jacques to ejaculate, when the watchful eye in my mind recognised that powerful asymmetrical contraction of his face. This confiscation of my old fantasies eventually produced a defensive reaction, but I still needed considerable perseverance and an effort of will for the sequences in which I myself was the protagonist to take back that zone of my imagination.

I cannot close this chapter on exchanges (which, like a silkworm's cocoon, covers and constitutes the sexual relation) without bringing up my only failed attempt at prostitution. When I heard mention of Madame Claude, I would always succumb to fanciful daydreams about high-class prostitution, envying Catherine Deneuve's character in *Belle de jour*, but I would have been completely incapable of negotiating the least exchange of this sort. People used to say that Lydie, the only woman I knew who took the initiative like a man during an orgy, had spent several days in a brothel in Palermo in order to earn enough money to throw a fantastic party for one of her friends. There was something mythical about this to me, and it left me stunned. I have made enough references to my shyness, to my characteristic of excessive reserve, for the reasons to be clear. To establish a mercenary

relationship, you have to negotiate an exchange of words or at least signals, the sort of complicity which forms the basis of all conversations and which would have seemed, to me, closely related to the preliminaries of seduction that I avoided. In both cases, in order to keep to your side of the deal, you have to take into the account your partner's attitudes and responses. Now, even at the first contact, I knew only how to focus on the body. It is only when I have, as it were, found my bearings with the body, when the grain of the skin and its particular pigmentation have become familiar to me, or I have learned to adjust my own body to it, that my attention could focus onto the person themselves, often – as I have said – to form a sincere and lasting friendship. But by then it would no longer be right to be asking for money.

I was short of it still. An old school friend wanted to help me out. A contact of hers had asked whether she would like to meet a woman who was keen to be introduced to very young women. She did not dare go herself but thought that I might be interested. She had an idea that doing that with a woman was less 'consequential' than with a man. I was given a rendezvous in a café in Montparnasse, with a suspicious go-between, a man of about thirty-five who looked like an estate agent. As a precaution, a friend watched me from a distance. I don't remember anything about the conversation or the proposed arrangements; I seem to think the guy was very careful to describe the woman we were meant to be meeting while I, probably unable to imagine myself cast as a prostitute, switched the roles in my mind's eye and imagined this woman as an ageing call girl, with bleached hair and loose, floaty underwear, lying back on a furry

bedcover with silent authority. Despite my naivety, I realised as soon as he took me to one of the little hotels I knew on the rue Jules-Chaplain that I would never see the woman. Perhaps the fact that he had spoken about her so much had immediately and definitively sent her back to the realms of imagination. The room was pleasantly cosy; he switched on both bedside lights but without bothering to switch off the overhead light, undid his zip straight away and asked me to suck him, in the same tone of voice as a man apologising for bumping into you on the metro even though he seems to think it's your fault. I carried out the job, only too relieved that I no longer had to face his rudeness. He lay down on the satin bedcover, he had a good hard erection and was easy to handle. I sucked him steadily without tiring, resting squarely on my knees which were perpendicular to his hips – one of the most comfortable positions. I was keen to finish with it because my thoughts were spinning round in my head. Should I say anything more about the woman we were meant to be meeting? That would be stupid. Should I ask for money for this fellatio? But shouldn't I have done that first? What was I going to tell the friend who was waiting for me? I was surprised by the sincere and youthful, abandoned expression on his face when he came, it was such a contrast to the way he behaved; it was also the only time in my life that I saw out the pleasure of a man I didn't like. I still have a clear image of the room as it was when we left it, the immaculate bedspread, the untouched chairs and the uncluttered surfaces of the little bedside tables under the lampshades. I denied it, but I could not disguise from the attentive friend who met me on a nearby terrace that I had made extensive use of my mouth. A blow-job,

especially if it is well done, bruises the insides of the lips. If you keep on going backwards and forwards with your mouth it's better to protect the activated member by curling your lips over your teeth – at least, that's the way I have always proceeded. 'Your lips are all swollen,' said my friend, telling me I was a fool. The young man who looked like an estate agent had followed me. He insulted us, claiming we had tried to con him in some way. I couldn't quite see how. He didn't press the point.

The teasing I have had for offering my body so easily but not knowing how to make money out of it! I was with men who were relatively well off, but I wasn't the sort to go through the acting out that would have been necessary if I were to gain any material advantage from them – advantages that they doubtless conferred on other girls. If I had to make a list – like heads of state who have to keep records of gifts received from ambassadors or foreign heads of state – the spoils would be meagre: a pair of sparkly orange stockings that I have never worn, three thick 1930s bangles in bakelite, a pair of off-white knitted shorts (definitely one of the first styles to come out in the winter 1970 prêt-à-porter collection) with a matching top, an authentic Berber wedding dress, a watch from a newsagent, a plastic brooch with a baroque geometric design typical of the early '80s, a necklace and a ring by Zolotas which, sadly, tarnished very quickly, a pearl-edged pareo, a Japanese brand electric dildo, along with three little metallic balls which are meant to be inserted into the vagina to stimulate during the act which never worked for me . . . I should add a contribution to the first dress I ever bought from a YSL boutique, a bath towel, also YSL, as well as extensive free dental care, and a loan

of several thousand francs that I never had to repay. My taxi and my air fare have always been paid for. 'You looked lost,' someone who knew me when I was very young tells me, 'and people just couldn't help themselves giving you 100-franc notes.' I must have gone on looking like that to men all my life, not like a woman who was after money, far from it, but like an adolescent who was no good at earning her living and who needed helping out with a bit of pocket money. I have, of course, excluded from this list all the presents Jacques gave me, given that our relationship was of a different order, and I consider as separate the works given to me by artists which I always think – as, indeed I do every time my professional interests have been closely linked with my sexual relationships – that they gratify the art critic in me just as much as, when that is their intention, they do the lover.

Always first times

We do not stick to the same sexual diet all the way through our lives! This may be due to our emotional circumstances (all our desires may be channelled through one person) but also to those times when we take stock of ourselves, thanks to changes which may have intervened in aspects of our lives not necessarily connected with love (moving house, illness, a new professional or intellectual environment . . .), when we find ourselves outside the track we had been following. I can think of two occasions when my sexual dispersion was stalled. When Jacques and I were preparing to live together, he wrote to tell me that we should hide absolutely nothing from each other, we

should not lie to each other. Now, it just happened that I had formed some relationships that I thought he would not be happy about. I managed to avoid a couple of meetings, to space out my orgies and to go through with the rest in a guilt-ridden state which I had hardly ever experienced before and which had an inhibiting effect, moderate but nonetheless real. On the other hand, one particular orgy which was in no way extraordinary, marked a turning point for me. I knew the couple who were our hosts, and – because he had just taken on the management of a big newspaper and she was a singer – I thought of them as parodies of characters from *Citizen Kane*. I had already fucked, if not both of them, certainly him. There were some distinguished guests, and they had split into two groups: one in a bedroom, the other on a sofa which stood rather oddly in the middle of a sitting room, lit by a chandelier. I was on the sofa, definitely glad to be in the group that was better lit, and active as I always was. I rather liked our host's dick, a short sturdy organ whose proportions made it a reduced model of his entire, compact body. Some people started to head for the bedroom, where a young woman buried in a deep eiderdown and waving her limbs in the air like a baby in its cot was hidden under the succession of broad backs that came and covered her, and whose cries could be heard all over the apartment. I observed this sort of extrovert behaviour with placid indifference. One of the participants expressed their admiration, saying she was 'really going for it', and I thought this was stupid. I went back to relax on the sofa. I thought that this young woman had taken up centre stage which, till then, had been mine, and that I should have been jealous of her, but my jealousy was lukewarm.

For the first time ever, I was pausing during one of those sessions in which I normally operated without stopping. And I appreciated that pause in the same way as I valued those moments when I withdrew into myself during a meal or meeting with friends. Of course I wondered about this new reaction of mine. The answer I found was that by constantly talking openly about these sort of practices with people who did or did not perform them; by commenting on them and interpreting them, usually with the arsenal of a lay psychoanalyst (which had the same effect on me as a cavalry regiment pitching up in the middle of a defiant Indian encampment); in short, by heading for a couch three times a week not to fuck but to talk about it, I had, without realising it – taken on the role not only of an active member but also of an observer.

And it was when I moved away from the centre of the spiral that I discovered something: my pleasure was never more intense than when it was the first time, not the first time that I made love with someone, but the first time we kissed; even the first embrace was enough. Obviously there were exceptions. Be that as it may, in most cases, even if what followed was not unpleasant, it was a bit like biting into the cone when you no longer have a mouthful of ice-cream to melt on your tongue, it had all the attraction of a painting that you admire but on which you are feasting your eyes for the fifteenth time. If I was taken by surprise, the pleasure was overwhelming. It is these situations which provide some of my clearest recollections of orgasms. I can cite them: late at night, crossing the huge lobby of an Intercontinental hotel; the elegant and distinguished assistant who has been travelling across the country with me for two weeks catches hold of my arm

when we have just said goodnight to each other, pulls me to him and kisses me on the mouth. 'In the morning, I'll come and see you in your room.' I can feel the spasm rising right up to my stomach and I set off towards the tiny little receptionists in the distance, twisting my ankle as I go. Another time, I dive down onto the carpet next to the master of the house who, slightly drunk, has crashed out on the floor next to some other guests, and who pulls me towards him by tugging under the neck of my sweater, and kisses me slowly with one of those cinema kisses that makes your head roll from side to side; this was not an evening destined to turn into an orgy, his wife was holding a conversation in the next room, one of his friends who was sitting on the floor like us and whose face happened to be on a level with ours, watched us in amazement. I go completely limp. And more: going to see the 'Dernier Picasso' exhibition at the Pompidou Centre with Bruno, with him there is always an element of chance. As he goes out of my field of vision while I go up to one of the paintings, his presence becomes all the more vivid and I am caught unawares by a brief but very distinct secretory discharge. As I carry on looking at the exhibition, I can feel the slimy patch on my tights shifting as I walk, first against the lips of my vagina, then against the swell of my inner thigh. Now, whereas in an early period of my life I didn't really care whether I experienced these feelings in more extensive contact, or during penetration, later on, when I had come to understand how singularly limited it was, I started to hope that that faraway tensing of an indefinable part of my lower abdomen and the famous wave that dissipated it could be repeated again and again as a relationship continued.

* * *

As I approached middle age I had two successive relation-ships, one easy-going, the other emotionally charged, but they nevertheless both followed a similar pattern: I took the time to take on board the desire I felt for the other, and this made that desire all the more pronounced; it culminated in passionate episodes of copulating during which my satisfaction was never as complete as it had been in the inaugural physical contact. For many years I faithfully maintained a friendship with the man who went to the Picasso exhibition with me, but it was threatened periodically by bursts of desire, sometimes aggressive, frustrated, not satisfactorily fulfilled, etc. It was my only truly chaotic experience. I would go to see him every day for weeks on end, then one day I would ring on the door and there would be no reply; the door would stay closed for several weeks, months even. And this would go on until my incredulous persistence was at last rewarded by a hoarse interjection on the telephone, authorising me to come before him once again. Probably because of this climate of uncertainty, I very frequently came instantly to orgasm with him. We would talk volubly, exchanging impressions of books, usually standing in a sparse interior that would have made a Quaker feel at home. Time would pass and I would move towards him. 'Do we want a little cuddle?' he would ask in the preoccupied but affectionate voice of an adult disturbed in their work by a child. Then his hand would push aside my knickers, and two fingers, four, would elicit a brief, anguished cry from me, because it was as much a sensation of suffocating surprise as of pleasure. He himself would derive pleasure from the fact that the passage was already dripping. We were generous

with our kisses and caresses. He made sweeping movements. If I was lying down, he would brush aside the sheet
with the same gesture that he used to stroke my breasts
throughout; I could lie straight and motionless on my
back while his palm swept up and down my entire length,
as if I had been but a sketch. When it was my turn to
attend to him, in contrast I explored him minutely, paying
special attention to the folds in his body, behind the ear,
his groin, his armpits, the parting between his buttocks. I
even scoured the furrowed lines in the crook of his hands.
Throughout these preliminaries, I kept thinking how
delicious it would be later on when he made up his mind
to turn me over and take me the way I like it, from behind,
when he grabbed my buttocks and smacked into them
loudly and abruptly with his hips. I particularly like it
when the dick jerks in and out; every three or four pumps,
a slightly harder thrust comes as a glorious surprise. And
yet it was only on a few exceptional occasions that I felt
the same intense pleasure as when his fingers opened
up the way. So I would start thinking that perhaps the
next time I would, and I busied myself – if I had to –
trying to force the resistance of that closed door, or of the
moral lesson.

Before that, I had had a relationship with the author of
the failed photographs taken in my office. He would
arrange to meet me either in a hotel near Gobelins or in a
disused apartment near the Gare de L'Est that was lent to
him. These meetings were always at an ungodly hour for
anyone trying to carry on professional activities that were
just a tad dependent on office hours: between eleven
o'clock and midday, between half past three and
four o'clock in the afternoon . . . the day before I could

already feel the anticipation of my snatch responding to the vibrating metro seat while I looked forward to our reunion. The feeling could be so maddening that I sometimes preferred to get off a few stops before my destination and to calm myself down by walking. That man could lick my snatch indefinitely. His tongue moved languorously, diligently parting all the folds of the vulva, knowingly describing circles round the clitoris then licking broadly like a young dog over the opening. The need to feel his organ breaching that gap became imperative. When at last he penetrated, just as softly and delving just as meticulously as he had with his tongue, my pleasure never managed to measure up to the escalation of desire.

Given the journeys I had to make to get to these rendezvous in only a short space of time, we sometimes missed each other. If he didn't turn up, I would stay lying on the bed, swinging my legs, my wanting wedged painfully between my legs, stopping me from closing them like a cross-strut. Afterwards I felt an apparently insurmountable oppression, it stopped me completing the day's tasks, going back to the office, making telephone calls, or making even the simplest decisions. How could I live a normal life until the next time we met, as if things were just fine? My gaping desire makes me feel like an abandoned wooden puppet, its stiff wooden legs spread helplessly, unable to move of their own free will. But happily this asthenia, which always hovers over me and varies in obsessiveness according to the situation, does not last. Even though I never consciously decide that it should be, the door of my office is always a perfectly impermeable screen, and I may well be dripping wet between

the legs (or could have been through any kind of event), I have the happy gift of being able to throw myself into my work with the same facility.

Would I ever have thought of writing this book which opens with a chapter called 'Numbers', if I had not once experienced being a minute satellite which suddenly left the orbit where it had been held by a whole network of connections but which now no longer govern it? The lift off happened in two stages. Firstly, there were times when I found satisfaction less frequently, and I coped with this frustration less tolerantly than I have just described. My excitement could rise to very high levels. The signs that I took as precursors of an overwhelming pleasure were that my lips would turn cold and I would get goose pimples (I will come back to these sensations in more detail later). If, as had more frequently become the case, the process ground to a halt, I would feel as if an insurmountable obstacle towered in front of me instead of the vast release I had hoped for. Each time, in the very moment when my partner was moving away and I was closing my legs, I searched, with the same stubborn resolve as when I am trying to describe something in an article, for a definition of the feelings inside me which I could not put into words. What name should I give to this singular emotion? That was the question I put to myself. It was in fact, I'm sure, a loathing of whoever was next to me at the time, but one which was obviously independent of my feelings for him the rest of the time. But at that moment this loathing filled me as closely and as fully as a liquid metal occupies a mould. I struggled obstinately to describe it to myself, and I remember sometimes comparing it to another form of

sculpture: Tony Smith's hermetic dice. Luckily, in the same way that the oppression that came over me after a failed rendezvous never lasted beyond the trip back in the taxi or the metro, this lacerating hatred put up no resistance to my reflex to slip off to the bathroom. And I think that it was in that position, as I ran a towel between my legs, that I first thought I ought to tell all about it.

For a period which I think lasted three years, perhaps four, and which constitutes what I think of as the second stage, my opportunities for sexual contact became rarer and, when they did arise, they were more or less of the kind described above. I also spent long weeks alone in Paris in the summer with my time divided between long working days and nights cut short both by the heat and by all the usual stress. That was when I delved through a pile of underwear and found the dildo I had been given years before and had never used. It has two different functions which can each be operated at two speeds. At one end there was a doll's head with a star on her forehead and a hairstyle that swept into wide curls around her neck, corresponding to the rolled edges of the glans. This head rotated in smaller or larger circles while something looking rather like a wild boar, attached half way down the shaft, quivered its extremely long tongue (either quickly or slowly) and was intended for the clitoris. The first time I used the thing, I came instantly, in one very long, perfectly identifiable, measurable spasm, and without needing to fantasize. I was completely taken aback. So an orgasm – an orgasm of the purest quality, even – could be achieved without perpetually having to return to that source, the thrill of the 'first time', by recreating various first times, and without even having time to convene my

mental repertoire of delivery boys and workmen. I very often wept after these speedy sessions. They combined a painfully violent pleasure with the sensuous delight of being alone that I have already evoked, here slightly heightened by a touch of bitterness. The contrast between something that corresponded so accurately with what is known as solitary pleasure and my usual taste for plurality was comic. One time I thought to myself that if I was going to have to speak out about 'the truth of the situation', the book should be called *The Sexual Life of Catherine M*. It made me laugh all by myself.

Although poorly provided for by nature in the first place, I now have the benefit of very healthy teeth, thanks to an excellent dentist who never once sent me a bill. The first time he greeted me as usual in his surgery and then showed me through to another waiting room, not the one in which I usually waited, a bigger room furnished quite differently with antique and not modern furniture, it was a bizarre, disturbing experience; it was as if, by passing through a familiar doorway, I had been magically trans-ported to a film set or into a dream. He left me there alone. Then burst into the room, pushed my clothes away from my breasts and my arse, caressed me and dis-appeared. Reappeared ten minutes later with a young woman. The three of us fucked. I only understood later that it was a double surgery with two waiting rooms lead-ing to two adjoining treatment rooms. Julien went from one to the other, treating one patient while the dressings on another dried. If I (or one of his other girlfriends, or a combination of the two) was in one of the treatment rooms, he could, with tremendous sleight of hand, rev up

his dick against one of our pussies, tidy it away, disappear through the connecting door, and then nip back. He usually ejaculated when he had scarcely penetrated. Alone he had designed and decorated this double surgery, working on it late into the evening after his last patients had left. At the weekend he competed in tennis tournaments to quite a high level. He would sometimes arrange to meet me in the afternoon, having booked a room in a five star hotel. I would check in, he would join me for a quarter of an hour and leave me the money to check out. I was fond of him. I was touched by the mysterious force that drove him in his tireless activity. And I identified with him to some extent, because I never stopped and as soon as I was in one place I wanted to be somewhere else, to see what was on the other side of the wall.

On a walk I hate coming back the same way that I set out. I study maps in minute detail to find a new way of getting to some piece of countryside, an edifice or a curiosity I haven't yet seen. When I went to Australia, the furthest I could get from home on this earth, I realised that my perception of this distance could be compared to the concept of having no sexual barriers. While I was thinking about this, I wondered whether the joy of parenthood belonged to the same family of emotions. Éric's ideas were in the same vein as these thoughts; he so cleverly adapted and changed the form our evenings took in the same way that (and these are his words) a 'tour operator' would. What mattered, he would point out, was to 'widen the available space'.

2. SPACE

Surely someone ought to write a study of the reasons why, during the course of their careers, eminent art historians (such as André Chastel and Giulio Carlo Argan) have focused increasingly on architecture? How did their analysis of the space represented in a painting mutate into an analysis of the way real space is organized? In my role as an art critic I might have felt more inclined to follow their example if I had not come across modern and contemporary pictorial works which could be said to inhabit the cusp between an imaginary space and the space in which we live, be they Barnett Newman's vast coloured expanses (Newman himself said: 'I declare space'), the radiant blues in the work of Yves Klein (who called himself the 'painter of space'), or even Alain Jacquet's topological surfaces and objects which juxtapose paradoxical abysses. What characterises these works is not the fact that they open space up, but that they both open and seal it – Newman with his closing zips, Klein by crushing his anthropometric forms, Jacquet by binding the ends of a Mobius ring. If you allow yourself to be led, it's like the boundless inner surface of a lung.

The Gates of Paris

The porte de Saint-Cloud car park borders onto the boulevard périphérique and in places is separated from it only by an openwork wall. All I had on were my shoes, having slipped off my raincoat whose lining iced my skin before getting out of the car. At first, as I have said, they rammed me up against a perpendicular wall. Éric saw me 'nailed by their pricks, like a butterfly'. Two men held me up under the arms and legs, while the others took it in turns hammering against my pelvis to which my whole person had been reduced. In these dicey situations, where there are many of them, men often fuck quickly and forcefully. I could feel the rugged surface of the breezeblocks digging into my shoulders and my hips. Even though it was late there was still some traffic. The thrumming of the cars, so close they seemed to brush past us, lulled me into the same torpor I feel waiting at airports. With my body both freed of all weight and curled up on itself, I retreated on myself. From time to time I would glimpse through my half-closed eyes the headlights of a car as they swept over my face. The men moved away from the wall and I felt myself simultaneously being levered up by two powerful jacks. A current fantasy, which had been nourishing my masturbation sessions for a long time, was to be taken to the dark foyer of a building by two strangers and to be impaled by both of them at the same time, like a sandwich, one in my cunt, the other up my arse, and here it found substance in an obscure atmosphere where reality and the images conjured in my mind fed off each other.

I must have come to, if I can call it that, when my body was returned to a more normal form of support. Someone

threw a coat over the bonnet of a car and lay me down on it. I'm familiar with this position which is not an easy one; I kept slipping and there was nothing to hold on to. I didn't always respond well to the different cocks that sought out my viscous canal. I was the focal point for a theatre of shadows, invisible until the headlights of a car threw their insipid light over the scene. From there I could make out the group scattered far and wide about me, I felt that those who had already shot their load completely lost interest in the ensuing proceedings. In front of me the silhouette of a much larger vehicle, probably a truck, perhaps had been chosen as a makeshift screen.

I remember when we arrived at the little stadium at Vélizy-Villacoublay how funny it seemed. The trip there had been so long, the leader of the convoy had been so mysterious about the destination, that when we came upon the place like a great clearing in the middle of a forest it just made us burst out laughing. It was a clear night. When you go to so much trouble to find a place, it's usually to choose somewhere less exposed, somewhere more appropriate for complicity! On top of that we all realised that we were going to be fornicating amid the ghosts of all the adolescents who came and played football there on Wednesday afternoons. Our guide responded to our questions by admitting that this had indeed been where he came for football training. He looked crestfallen, as if he had been forced to admit to a long-standing fantasy. Who hasn't dreamed of polluting some ordinary and innocent place they know with a bit of nooky? The group took refuge under the sloping terraces, because it goes so against human nature to copulate in full view of the horizon or in too expansive a space. On the whole, we

protect ourselves less from other people's gazes which can constitute an even more definite barrier than their bodies. People who fuck on the beach on moonlit summer nights think about the intimacy of their situation, and this cuts them off from the immensity around them. Our group was too big and too spread out to create that sort of intimacy itself. I took the cocks standing up, hanging on to some of the posts under the terraces, with my dress lifted up (I didn't want to take everything off because it was so cold, but my buttocks were still completely exposed). Because I have a very supple waist, I am well suited to this position. So this circle of joyful activity continued, forming a perimeter around my outstretched arse, while I gazed absently through the frame of floorboards to the empty pitch.

I think I must have ended up naked. There was some joke about the available changing rooms: might as well make the most of them. They were behind a little shed which must also have served as a bar because it had a counter along the front. I lay down there for a while, taking ambivalent pleasure in being manhandled and inspected like a choice piece of merchandise. I wriggled about and breathed in deeply the damp night air. The shed roof extended into an awning over the counter. The wooden walls were clean and smooth, with no notices pinned to them, the general impression was simplicity bordering on minimalism like those theatre sets that set designers dream up that are like working drawings, far removed from reality. I was treated to some final fondlings, to a few licks on my vulva offered at just the right height and then, as the journey there had been so long, the cars soon set off again.

Many of these adventures take place at night and this is obviously because it is then that the public places that allow you to gather in large groups and that provide amusing stages (for spectacles for which they were not intended) are more accessible and are not usually so closely guarded. That is how one of Éric's girlfriends came to know the icy but stimulating sensation of a huge belt buckle against her buttocks when the couple and a group of bikers had met to their mutual satisfaction in the Bois. People also think that darkness protects them. But for some people, myself included, it at the same time opens the space around them up to infinity by making it limitless. The tall hedge a few metres away is no longer an obstacle. In fact, you hardly ever find complete darkness, and people actually usually prefer the vagueness of half light. I myself would like total blackout because I could then experience the pleasure of sinking into a sea of undifferentiated flesh. On the other hand, I know how to make the most of harsh light too, because the initial blindness and inability to identify its source dissolve and blur the frontiers of bodies. In other words, I am not afraid of being glimpsed unawares because my body is but a mingling part of the air around it and the continuum of other bodies connected to it. I, therefore, can't even conceive that anyone is looking in from the outside.

When Bruno and I were out for a walk after dinner one night, some intuition drove us to an area of grass on the edges of the Bois de Vincennes. It was a half-hearted lawn, bordered by a strip of concrete rather like a pavement, and with sparse, dry grass. There was a bench there. We started pressing up against each other on it, not really caring that the place was lit by a street light and quite a

way from the edge of the forest. It could have been a scene from a film in the late forties, when the camera pans out and isolates the characters in a halo of light. When Bruno lifted up my dress and started to bring me off energetically, the trees were out of focus. Even though we weren't really aware how unwise this might turn out to be, we didn't talk and we did try to make the space we occupied smaller by making only brief movements and taking it in turns to attend to each other. While his fingers delved between my thighs, I stayed curled up against him with my legs folded up as tightly as the position of my arms would allow. I had kept my top on. When it was my turn to bend over the bulge in his jeans, he sat motionless with his head on the backrest of the bench, his body stiff as a board. I undertook a conscientious blow-job, avoiding any changes of rhythm so as to prevent any sudden reactions. Suddenly, a second, powerful light came on in the distance, aimed towards us. For a moment, we froze expectantly, unable to identify exactly what this light was or where it was coming from. One of Bruno's characteristic responses was to let himself be sucked off passively, almost as if it was against his will, sometimes even interrupting, then starting the process up again without any warning by grabbing his prick and aiming it at my mouth, as if he would almost have preferred entering by force. That is what he did then, bringing my head down by pushing on the nape of my neck. My lips and hand resumed their repetitive movement. None of the things that this brutal illumination of our soldered forms implied actually happened. The light that shone on the side of my face was so bright that it dazzled me through closed eyelids. I saw the peaceful fellation through to its conclusion

in the half-silence of our breathing and with the black and gold splashes of light dancing before my eyes. Then we went home, sharing an amused feeling of perplexity we barely discussed. Had we been in the headlights of a car? A police car or a voyeur's? Had a faulty floodlight come back on by itself? I never found an explanation for that perfectly focused light.

Open air

If I heard anyone say of me 'fucking comes to her as easily as breathing', I would agree more than willingly because the expression could be taken literally. My first sexual experience, and many others since, took place in circumstances which could lead one to believe that oxygen has an aphrodisiac effect on me. My nudity feels more complete to me out in the open than in a closed room. When the surrounding temperature, whatever it may be, can be felt by an area of skin it doesn't normally reach, such as the small of the back, the body no longer presents an obstacle to the air, it is penetrated by it and is, therefore, more open, more receptive. When the atmosphere which embraces the vastness of the world adheres to the surface of my skin like a myriad tiny suction pads, my vulva also feels as if it has been drawn out and dilates deliciously. If a gentle wind blows across its threshold, the feeling is amplified: the labia feel bigger than ever, gorged with the air brushing past them. I will speak later, and in more detail, about erogenous zones, but I can say even now that even the gentlest attention to the oft ignored area which links the anal depression to the triangle where the labia

meet – that underrated rut between the arsehole and the beginning of the cunt – is guaranteed to subjugate me, and that feeling the air against that part of my body is more intoxicating than high altitude. I like opening up my buttocks and my legs to the flow of air.

There must be a fairly general intrinsic link between the idea of moving in space, of travelling, and the idea of fucking, otherwise the widespread expression 'having it away' would not have been invented. Taking into account all these factors, terraces, roadsides, stretches of open country, and any space designed merely to be crossed, such as concourses and car parks, all of these are places (or non-places as Marc Augé calls them) where it feels good to me to follow their example and be open.

The first time I took all my clothes off in front of several pairs of eyes, I was in the middle of a garden surrounded by a mesh fence. You already know about this. I have also referred to that other garden which was in a particularly interesting site overlooking the sea. The garden stretched out in front of the house and, even though we were in the Midi, there was very little shade. Right at the front, an area of paving served as a sun terrace. We fucked there endlessly even in the heat of the day. Anyone flying overhead would have been amused, as you can be from an aeroplane, by the juxtaposition of contrasting scenes. It is always funny seeing the frantic streams of traffic on the outskirts of the city you have just left but also, in the same glance, seeing the emptiness of the surrounding countryside. It isn't just that there is an abrupt join between these two images, running along the seam of a motorway, but that they represent two conflicting things which know nothing of each other in an almost hostile way; the

speeding cars drawn magnetically to the city centre seem to look down on the solitary vehicle fleeing to the countryside. Up above Saint-Jean-Cap-Ferrat you could have seen a little agglomeration of human bodies a little way away from a big house – abandoned for enigmatic reasons – but very close to a road where the cars heading for the cape and those returning from it passed each other continuously. It would have been difficult to make out the boundary which produced the mutual indifference between this group of people and these cars. The very low grey stone wall at the bottom of the garden threw very little shadow and it would not have been obvious from the air that the road was several metres below the level of the garden. That particular summer I had two acolytes: a lesbian girlfriend and one of those girls met by chance on an outing and who, because we liked her, became part of the group for the holidays. We spent very little time in the villa, except to sleep and to prepare meals, and our assiduous sunbathing had turned the terrace end of the garden into one of those focal meeting places that all households elect even when they are not necessarily the most convenient spots! New visitors arrived every day. With some, although of course not all, a bit of sunbathing or an afternoon siesta would see some developments. It was a sort of casual summer activity, like going out in a boat. Judith, who preferred women, still accepted anyone of either sex who showed willing with slightly detached good humour. She was a big girl, with the sort of body that is seen as beautiful because it is – as they say – all in proportion, fashioned by a pantograph that simply amplified the blueprint of a slim girl. Her breasts were not heavy but shaped like cones with perfectly central nipples.

The other girl had big, drooping breasts above a waist you could encircle with two hands. As I lay on my back, shifting my head away from the shoulder obscuring my view, I could see her thin frame silhouetted against the sky, and the heavy teardrops of her breasts undulating in the wake of her movements. I thought that her body couldn't possibly contain what she must have buried into it as she sat astride a particularly well endowed member of the group. She too had an angelic disposition, and we were an amicable trio with a constant appetite and without aggro. There was another girl, who stood head and shoulders above all of us and who coiled herself up when she fucked as if trying to leave more room for the other smaller body ramming her so zealously, and I remember that once she burst a string of pearls with the pressure of her congested neck. Nothing ever disturbed the unspooling of those compact segments of afternoon, their rhythm slowed further by the humming of the traffic absorbed into the buzzing of insects and, even though the clattering of those pearls on the ground was barely discernible and this girl in her rapture didn't moan any louder than anyone else, I was surprised by such a transport of ecstasy. I started to think: 'Can a woman really experience such overwhelming pleasure that her body undergoes this sort of external transformation?' I was at my leisure to watch the fixed grimaces on some men's faces or, on others, the distant, absent mask, as their bodies reached maximum tension, when (in, for example, the classic position) they arch from the small of their back right up to their necks, peeling away from their partner's body with the same robust uplift as the prow of a schooner over the sea. But I watched women much less and, without the mirror they

could have held up to me, I had no image of my own body at such moments even though I am not short on narcissistic tendencies. I knew how to take up the right position and what moves to make; beyond that, everything was diluted into sensations that I didn't connect with any visible manifestations. If I can put it like this, these feelings didn't take on a physical form, even less so in the suave pleasures of the open air. There were times when I liked to withdraw, to detach myself from the great writhing on the beach mattresses, and to lie down on the wall just as I was. The light was too bright to stare up at the sky. If I turned my head to one side, the horizon was on a level with my eyes; on the other side I had to close them because the light bounced off the pale paving stones.

Now here is a position I really like: arching my back down to facilitate access to my pussy so that it can be well and truly hammered from behind while contemplating a wide panorama. As Jacques has a predilection for impromptu fucks in the countryside, I'm not deprived of these opportunities. In the region where we spend our holidays lots of tracks lead to dead ends in the vineyards. We come to one of these dead ends, high up and abandoned, and, avoiding the brambles, pick our way to the dry stone wall. Because I don't want to take my trainers off, I stretch my knickers wide as I take them off so as not to dirty them when I pull them over my feet. I am wearing a shirt dress which I have unbuttoned and Jacques lifts it up over my back. With outstretched arms and clutching my knickers in one hand, I lean precariously against the rickety stones. In these circumstances there are not always any preliminaries; Jacques introduces himself into the vulva which gradually opens up, squeezing the

spare flesh under my waist firmly in his hands. With my head hanging down I can look into the darkened room of my body as it bends over itself, my breasts hanging down and swinging, the regular undulations of my stomach and, at the end of the narrow gallery, where the light appears again, a little bit of the crumpled surface of his balls and, intermittently, the base of his member. Watching the very short, very measured coming and going heightens my excitement as much as if not more than the movement itself.

I curve my back still further and lift my head to offer more resistance to Jacques' hips as they smack more sharply against my arse. On the slopes of the little hill we're overlooking, the vines have been replaced by scrub. When my cunt has been sensitised to its very depths, I just have to close my eyelids and, through my eyelashes, I can see the village of Latour-de-France over to the right. I still have the faculty to think to myself: 'There's Latour-de-France' and to appreciate not for the first time its picturesque position on an outcrop of rock in the middle of the valley. The landscape spreads wider before me. I recognise the moment when my pleasure won't go any further (when I've climaxed, however intense it may have been) and I let Jacques come; he paces his thrusts more slowly until the final three or four of orgasm, while my mind abandons itself to another fulfilling pleasure: floating freely, it hovers over and follows the contours of each hill, clearly distinguishing each from the next, and sinking into the inky magic of the mountains in the background. I so love this constantly changing landscape, revealed as a series of planes falling heavily in front of each other, and right there and then I am happy to be flooded and

overflowing with cum welling up in the depths of my belly.

Céret is a noble-looking town set in countryside which still has a wild quality. There are very good restaurants there. Having arrived late one afternoon, too early to sit down and eat straight away, Jacques and I decide to climb up to a sandy track some four or five metres wide. It slopes gently and the ground is level so I don't even have to take off the very high black patent shoes I'm wearing for the occasion. In the near dusk the contrast between the white path and the high dark vegetation bordering onto it is more striking. On the valley side, breaks in the foliage afford glimpses over the overlapping expanses of rustic tiles which contradict the perception you have of the town when you walk between its elegant eighteenth-century facades, along its avenues roofed by 30-metre plane trees. You would think that the entire plain had been pushed by the sea like a vast barge, and had forced the town to huddle itself against the mountainside. We stop and, standing one in front of the other, pick out other villages as if we were looking at a map. Cautious men take you first by the shoulders and your breasts, tickling around the base of your neck with their lips. Jacques always starts by taking hold of the buttocks. He immediately grasps the fact that there is nothing under the designer, dog-tooth check, bustier dress which I shed in one swift movement as if sloughing off a skin. He slips in from behind, gently exploring my pussy with his little probe, but not trying to penetrate. I press my back against him. The air temperature is perfect. A correlation develops between the space around us and the way his hands wander expansively over my chest and stomach. I do, however, avoid these caresses

because, even when his dick has really stiffened, I don't take it in my cunt before devoting just the briefest fellation to it. At last I offer my rump. Balancing on my heels, with my legs slightly bent to be at the right height for the lovely, lubricated tip, I put my hands onto my tensed thighs and spread out my fingers. It is quite a tiring position to maintain without any other support. But what a good poking I had that evening, my rear end grasped between his hands, pinioned and kneaded, with my top half thrust forward over the Roussillon plain as it slowly dissolved! I can clearly remember then thinking to myself, in one of those hyper-conscious states crystallised by pleasure, that one day I would have to find a way of putting into words the extreme sensation of joy when two bodies that are joined together feel as if they are unfurling. To understand this, you just have to imagine those shots you see in films about the wonders of nature, which use accelerated footage to show the petals of a rose suffused with oxygen and methodically smoothing themselves out.

We are all subject to social laws and under obligation to family rites: we conform to what is now called the 'enterprise culture', and even in the intimacy of our sexual lives we instigate habits and institute a code for the exclusive use of two people – a 'couple culture', you could say. So open-air copulation forms part of Jacques' and my 'couple culture'. In the same way that I have put coloured drawing pins into a globe to show the places I have visited, I could tick off on detailed maps the ruins and the rocks, the bends in the road and the clumps of trees where someone looking through binoculars could have stumbled across the quiverings of a minute two-headed silhouette. Early one morning, against the off-white coloured rocks

of a steep mountainside, me with my body braced in its usual position, clutching the narrow trunk of a young tree with sparse foliage, and with my shorts barely lifted, we are joined by a man: are we in the area for a holiday? Have we lost our way? Once he has moved away, we speculate that – to avoid possible burglaries – he must have the job of guarding the hermitage which was in fact the reason for our climb. Another chapel, this one in ruins, but still with high walls standing proud on a flat plateau with a criss-cross of little walls around it, those of the long crumbled sacristy where it's good to walk and imagine its inhabitants, as in an ancient ruin. The short nave is in full sunlight, the choir in the shade, the altar of dark grey stone is intact. I lie down on it, too high off the ground to be taken. While Jacques leans over and arouses me with a few playful licks, I keep my eyes wide open, gazing at the sky defined by the ridge of black walls; I could be at the bottom of a well. Once again we end up upright, in a tiny space just big enough for the two of us, and whose use we can't really guess. A corridor? A recess for a long lost statue?

Other ruins, other razed spaces, this time a huge fortified farm and its outbuildings, and the plateau that – from its steep banks – it still seems to defend. I should point out another particular of our 'couple culture': between a third and a half of our sexual embraces are an interlude in a photo shoot. On this occasion the latter was long and complicated. I've brought a variety of clothes, some very fragile and I'm afraid of catching them in the bushes and the piles of stone. Same worry when I have to change clothes between poses, especially with a silk chiffon dress which corkscrews in the wind. Jacques is going for light

contrasts and gets me to explore every nook and cranny of the ruins. I walk carefully over the stony ground because my shoes have sharp, high heels and pointed toes which hurt. I also have to avoid the goat droppings because, before we turned this ruin into a photographic studio, a herd of goats used it for grazing. More than once, I climb the walls barefoot, then Jacques hands me the shoes and I slip them on for a few poses. For each pose, I have to find a compromise between the precise position Jacques asks for (down to the last centimetre of how much pubic hair is showing and how wide the thighs are spread, or how tightly the see-through top fits) and the pain in my feet as I try to balance, or my buttocks positioned next to clumps of brambles. While my gaze wanders over the 360° of the panorama, my body is reduced to an extremely narrow margin of movement. Once in position, I obey my instructor reluctantly. Then, before the film runs out, I in turn ask him to take a last few pictures of me walking naked along the wide path which slopes gently back down to the car, left in the middle of the plateau. After so many constraints, I need to move forwards in the hot air like an animal of the savannah.

The open door of the four-wheel drive will be an unnecessary screen; we've already seen that there isn't a car anywhere near the only inhabited house on the plateau, and its inhabitants must, therefore, be out. Is it because of the two hours spent within reach of thousands of nature's lowly little assaults, or perhaps because of my hovering suspicion that Jacques has recently grabbed other arses than mine behind this metal screen? My vagina isn't ready. In these instances, I separate the lips and moisten them

hastily with saliva, surreptitiously deposited on the tips of my fingers. There will still be a bit of resistance, but the glans will scarcely have forced its entry before the secretory mechanism will be set in motion and soon the whole cock will have assumed its place in a suitably moist cunt. I think that first I put one leg forward and pushed it against the running board, perhaps to open the vulva a little further, but it has to be said that, if I have to turn my back on my partner, I like nothing better than jerking my arse against him. To do this I have to have a supple waist and it's better to have your feet together. The more I stick my arse out towards him, the more I can fantasise that my arse has taken on the autonomy normally attributed to the head because it is the seat of thought which lives on independent from the rest of the body; and, thus, my arse is the counterpart of my head. While I sought out Jacques' organ, as if I were going to yoke it up to myself, I caught a glimpse of myself in the rear-view mirror, with my body connected to his and to the whole background. When I see myself in the act, my features seem devoid of expression. There must be moments when, like everybody else, I make faces, but when I chance across a reflection in a window or mirror, I don't look the way I think I am at that moment: my gaze is vague, looking inwards as it would onto an open space, but trusting, as if trying to find some point of reference.

The practice of open-air fucking became anchored in the way Jacques and I organised our lives right from the beginning of our relationship. A visit to his grandmother in a nondescript little village in the Beauce region, included a compulsory stop-off by the side of the road. He would park the 2CV on the verge, we would nip through

a hedge and find a field rising gently up to the horizon, and disappear into the grass. We really had to wriggle about to get out of our tight-fitting jeans. I would put my jacket down on the grass under my head for fear of insects, and Jacques protected the small of my back. Having not spent my adolescence in the countryside, I took naive pleasure in these hasty couplings of just two half-bodies; suddenly my legs and buttocks were not at the same temperature as the upper half of my body which was still clothed, and Jacques somehow had to manage with his underpants and the waist of his trousers hampering his thighs. There is a childish pleasure in showing those naked parts getting off, as if the swaddled other half were their alibi.

The Mediterranean landscape in which we took to living for several weeks a year is very rugged, but its low vines and its scrubland offer hardly any hiding places and even fewer natural beds. There isn't any grass and, as there are no trees, I often had to hang onto the windowless door of an abandoned car or to the uprights at the opening to a pigsty, my rear end jutting out all the further as my eyes and nose struggled with the smell of putrefaction.

We often used a track which led up to a field of young vines planted in crushed white rocks, a track now almost disappeared since we stopped using it. We identified some favourite spots along that track as time went by. Halfway up, just before it became more steep, it widened out onto a sandy platform and all along one side the sand gave way to an outcrop of curved rocks; you could have fun imagining that they were the backs of hippopotamuses breaking through the muddy waters of a river which also

deposited dented old petrol cans and broken pallets. I could lie down on the smooth surface of the rocks with Jacques leaning on his arms like an awning above me, giving me a few quick thrusts with his member. But it wasn't easy for him to get deep enough in this position. The solution was for me to turn round and get onto all fours, like the Roman she-wolf on her pedestal, receiving the very special offering of her devoted priest.

Further up there was a hairpin bend in the track. On one side there was a ditch which acted as a dumping ground and, every time we passed, we noticed that its contents had mysteriously changed: the carcasses of agricultural machinery, the Cyclops heads of washing machines, etc. On the other side a pale coloured rock ran along it for several metres, shear like a wall. Despite the intensity of reflected light, it was one of our elected stopping points, because there too the smooth rocks comfortably accommodated the palms of my hands, but also – and why not? – because we unconsciously liked to feel that our bodies came from the jumble around us. As there were no leaves to wipe ourselves with, and we didn't always think to come equipped with handkerchiefs I would stay turned towards my rock for a few moments, with my legs apart, watching the cum falling from my pussy onto the ground in a lazy drool the same whitish colour as the rocks. Further up again, on top of the plateau, the track ended in a huddle of trees where the remains of picnics sometimes mingled with the dry bushes, and which might have offered a bit more shade. But we stopped there only a few times. You had to get there in the first place and, when we did, the business had often already been seen to. Jacques would not have been

able to resist the undulating buttocks under the skirt or shorts in front of him, their movement as regular as breathing, marking out the rhythm as I walked; while I would be making the ascent absorbed in the thought of his gaze on me, giving me plenty of time to ready my snatch whose opening I can only compare to a baby bird's tirelessly gaping beak.

For some indiscernible reason, then, the 'couple culture' I am describing played out its adventures mainly in bucolic settings. It's true that fucking in sunken tracks is less risky than in the porches of buildings. That is not to say that, with other lovers, both Jacques and I did not use urban locations. But metro station corridors (where an employee uses the jostle of the crowd to brush imperceptibly over my buttocks – a tacit invitation to join him in a box-room cluttered with pails and brooms) and little cafés in the suburbs (where joyless men take me in turns on a bench seat in the back room) are places I have visited with Jacques only in my imagination. And even then was I taking him there? I have stopped doing it now, but there was a time when I liked to redecorate the room with my elaborate fantasies, gradually detailing the settings and the positions I adopted, in an almost questioning tone of voice because I would wait for Jacques' acquiescence, which he would grant in a neutral voice and with the indifferent spontaneity of someone who's thinking about something else (but he was probably only feigning indifference), while his tool filed sweetly and steadily. I draw two conclusions from these points.

The first is that, within a couple, each person brings with them their own fantasies and desires, and that these combine into shared habits which then modulate and

adjust to each other and, depending on the extent to which each partner wants them to be realised, cross the barrier between dream and reality without losing any of their intensity. My obsession with numbers found its realisation when I practised group sex with Claude and with Éric, because that was how their own desires fused with mine. On the other hand, I did not feel any frustration at never taking part in group sex with Jacques (even when he told me he had done so without me); it must simply be that that was not the way of our shared sexuality. It was enough for me to tell him about my adventures and to intuit that they found some resonance in his fantasies, just as it was enough for him that I was a willing accomplice for his photographic reportages in those variously polluted landscapes, and an exhibitionist ready to expose herself for his lens – even if my narcissism would have preferred more flattering backgrounds and more stylised portraits . . .

The second conclusion is that natural spaces do not feed the same fantasies as urban spaces. Because the latter is by definition a social space, it is a territory in which we express a desire to transgress codes with our exhibitionist/voyeuristic impulses; it presupposes the presence of others, of fortuitous looks to penetrate the aura of intimacy which emanates from a partially naked body or from two bodies soldered together. Those same bodies out under the clouds, with only God as their witness, are looking for the opposite sensation; not to make others come into the pocket of air in which their rapid breathing mingles, but, thanks to their Edenic solitude, to let their pleasure spread as far as the eye can see. The illusion there is that their ecstasy is on the same scale as this expanse, that the body

that houses them is dilating to infinity. Perhaps the tipping into unconsciousness known as the *petite mort* is felt more keenly when the bodies are in contact with the earth, teeming with invisible life and in which everything is buried. Granted, most of my masturbatory fantasies take place in urban settings (apart from those already mentioned, the following is often called up: a man in a packed metro train presses his flies up to my buttocks and manages to hitch my clothes up enough to slip his dick in; his manoeuvre is not lost on other men who move through the crowds to take his place; the carriage is divided between those taking pleasure and those taking offence, the factions start arguing . . . : go find a more Parisian fantasy!), and I managed to make do with the hard shoulders of main roads and the car parks of the capital. Even so, when all is said and done, I think I prefer vast open spaces. In fact, at night cities give you the illusion of vastness. When Claude and I started living together, we would get home late to our little apartment in the suburbs, I would walk ahead of him and, without any warning, would lift my skirt up over the naked globe, not as an invitation for him to fuck me there (I don't think we ever did), nor to shock a potential passer-by, but to breathe in the road around me, a cool balm for my quivering crack. In fact, I wonder whether the men of trees and car parks, by their sheer numbers and their shadowy nature, aren't made of the same substance as space, whether I didn't just rub myself up against shreds of the same fabric as air though with a slightly closer weave. More specifically: I have an unrivalled ability to find my way on an unfamiliar road. Perhaps the aptitude to pass from one man to another within a group, or to navigate –

as I did at certain times in my life – between a number of different relationships, perhaps they belong to the same family of psychological predispositions as a sense of direction.

Different towns, different men

Throughout the first few years of my adult life, my sexual experiences were intimately linked with the need to escape. That need even instigated them. It was when I ran away from home for the first time that I lost my virginity. I had argued with my parents yet again. Claude, who I did not yet know, had rung at the door of our apartment to let me know that a friend I was meant to be meeting had been delayed. He asked me to go out with him. In the event, his Renault 4 took us all the way to Dieppe. We set up the tent on the edge of the beach.

Some time later I fell in love with a student from Berlin. We did not make love together (he was a cautious young man, and I had not made any demands), but the long sturdy frame of his body lying next to mine and his big white hands sent me into ecstasies. I wanted to go and live in West Berlin. The wide Kudam leading all the way up to the gleaming blue cathedral, and the parks of that great city – even though it was divided at the time – fuelled my dreams. And then the student wrote and told me that it would not be sensible for us to be committed when we were so young. Another excuse to run away, again with Claude (whom I still saw) and his Renault 4. Destination Berlin, to talk with the boy who wanted to break up with me. Attempt to cross the border between East and West

Germany which failed because I did not have the necessary papers. So the student came as far as the frontier to talk it through, and my first romance came to an end in a cafeteria in a huge car park in the middle of a forest, amidst queues of people and queues of cars waiting to pass the wooden sentry boxes.

Unfortunately, I retained this propensity to flee without warning for many years, which was neither fair to the man I was living with at the time, nor to those who had brought me there, or those I had gone to meet, and would abandon to return home. This restlessness was partly due to the febrile interest that we had (Claude, Henri, a few others and myself) towards the New World of sex, an attitude which would sometimes make one of us strike out as an individual. The unspoken law expected the pioneering scout to tell about their adventures on their return. Which, of course, was not always the case, hence the mixture of oil and water which constituted, on the one hand, our disparate desires and, on the other, our libertarian minds. Going away for two days with a man I barely knew, or, as I did for several years, carrying on a relationship with a colleague who lived in Milan, was just as worthwhile for the journey and the change of scenery as it was for the promise of being bedded, touched and shafted in a way I was not accustomed to. If it had been possible, I would have liked to have woken up each morning to the shadows of an as yet unexplored ceiling and to have climbed out of the sheets and stayed for a few moments in the no man's land of an apartment in which I had forgotten overnight which corridor led to the bathroom. At times like that, it is the other body that you leave behind, a body you may have known only a few hours,

but which during those hours has nourished you with its solid presence and its smell, it is that body which provides you with the ineffable well-being of familiarity. How many times have I thought, as I fantasised languidly about the life of high class whores, that that was one of the advantages of their job. As for the journey itself, the lapse of time we inhabit when we are no longer in one place but not yet in another, can be a source of pleasure measured on the same scale as erotic pleasure. In a taxi when all the bustle that precedes departure suddenly falls away, or descending into that semi-conscious state while waiting at an airport, I can sometimes feel that instantly recognisable sensation of a giant hand which from inside my body, squeezes my entrails and draws from them a sensuous delight which irrigates my every extremity, exactly like when a man looks at me in a way which implies he has me in his sights.

In spite of this, I have never used the frequent, long-distance journeys necessitated by my work to collect lovers. I fucked infinitely less when my timetable was more flexible than it is in Paris, and when I could have made the most of those casual relationships with no tomorrows. However hard I try to remember, I can think of only two men that I have met on a journey and with whom I had some form of sexual relationship during the journey itself. And when I say relationship, there was only one instance each time, between breakfast and the first meeting of the morning with one, and during what was left of the night with the other.

There are two explanations. Firstly, right at the beginning of my career a more experienced female colleague had led me to understand that symposia, seminars and

119

other meetings held in seclusion with people who were temporarily cut from their ties were God-given opportunities for furtive comings and goings up and down hotel corridors. I was used to sexual rendezvous of a more advanced nature; nevertheless this shocked me to the same extent as the shapeless clothes people wear to show that they are on holiday when they would usually be very particular about their appearance. With the intransigence of the newly converted, I believed that fucking – and by that I meant fucking frequently and willingly whoever was (or were) the partner (or partners) was a way of life. If not, if this thing were only permitted when certain conditions were met, at pre-determined times, well then it was carnival! (A little aside to put this severe verdict into context. We no longer need to prove that our sexual tendencies can turn inside out like an old umbrella, and the device that protects us when the wind blows with reality can flip the other way and leave us to get soaked in the squalls of our fantasies. Once again in this book, I am bringing together fact and fantasy, in this case to expose a pleasing antinomy: despite the moral stance I have just expressed, I have often been aroused by imagining myself as a spunk bag for a group of stressed executives at a meeting, they would each dump their load on me secretly, at the back of a hotel bar, even in a phone box, with the receiver in one hand as they carried on their ritual conversation with their wife: 'Yes darling, it's going well, it's just the food that's not . . .' etc. That's a surefire stellar scenario for me to get off on in a state of complete degradation.)

In the realms of reality, though, the exotic adventures of this speleologist of Parisian car parks can be dealt with in

just two paragraphs. The assistant who had so emphatically drawn me to him right in the middle of the hotel foyer
did indeed come and wake me up the following morning.
Very fair, he had let me rest after our many journeys – we
had been going across Canada – over the last few days. He
pushed his hips calmly. I let him get on with it without
much conviction, but I encouraged him almost as a
professional would, choosing however a vocabulary that
was more amorous than obscene. Afterwards he said,
quite unaffectedly, that he had been thinking about it for
several days, but that he had waited until the end of the
trip so as not to disturb our work. We worked together
again a number of times. He never made the slightest
gesture of sexual invitation again, and neither did I. It was
the first time that a sexual exchange that had started with
someone whom I was to see again did not continue, did
not naturally fertilize the soil of our relationship as friends
and colleagues. It has to be said that I was at a stage in my
life where I was trying with limited success, if not to be
faithful, at least to limit myself. I thought that there might
be the excusable transgressions permitted to people who
were not libertines. It was the only time in my life that I
vaguely regretted a sexual act.

A Brazilian adventure left me with more complex feelings. I had just arrived in Rio de Janeiro for the first time
and, of all the telephone numbers I had been given, this
artist was the only person to reply. As luck would have it,
he was very familiar with an area of French cultural
history which was my field, and we stayed up very late,
chatting on a gloomy terrace in Ipanema. Several years
went by, he came to Paris, I went back to Brazil a couple
of times. In Sao Paulo, as we came away from a party for

the Biennale, we took the same taxi. He gave the address of my hotel. Without taking my eyes off the taxi-driver's neck, I drummed my fingers lightly on his thigh. He gave the address of his hotel. The bed stood by a bay window and street signs outside threw blocks of yellow light across it as in a Hopper painting. He did not cover me, he sowed parts of his body like gentle seeds over mine, reassuring himself that I was there with his hands, his lips, his penis, as well as his forehead, his chin, his shoulders and legs. I felt good, and then was drowned in the depths of a migraine which terrified him. I could hear him whispering about the time, about all that time. There was no second time with him, either. Later, in another taxi, in Paris this time, as I watched rather than listened to him speaking to me attentively, I was overcome by an intense feeling of joy: I was thinking about the geographical distance between us, the long intervals of time between our meetings which were nevertheless regular – sometimes, when in Rio, I might just give him a quick call; and I thought of that single occasion when time and space had come together, and their union had formed a perfect architecture.

The other explanation for the limitations in my adventures while travelling is connected with a subject I raised in the first chapter. I liked to discover – on condition that I had a guide. I liked it if a man was introduced to me by another man. I would leave it up to the relationship the one had with the other, rather than having to think about my own desires and how to satisfy them. In fact, feeling desire and having sexual relations were almost two separate activities; I could want a man very much and nothing ever actually happen without feeling

any frustration. I was a dreamer, a gifted fabulist; a major part of my erotic life was lived like that, heightened by the friction on my vulva, held between my thumb and index finger. Copulating really answered to a wider necessity: to carve a smooth path for myself in the world. As I have had the opportunity to illustrate, I was living in the comfort of a family-like complicity. Something you do not get when you arrive for the first time (and without any specific tips) in some distant city.

With many men, it is their houses that I remember before anything else. That is not an excuse to under-estimate other memories that I have of them, it is rather that these cannot be dissociated from their background, and that it is a spontaneous reconstruction of this back-ground which brings back a moment of affectionate friendship or the details of the geometry of bodies. The reader may well have realised: I quickly take in the setting. Where my most intimate slit has given access, I have opened my eyes wide too. Very young, I learned to use this method, amongst others, to find my way around Paris. An architect friend whom I used to visit in his Parisian *pied-á-terre* on the top floor of a new building, so high up that the view from the bed dived straight into the sky, once commented that from my place in the rue Saint-Martin on the Rive Droite to his at the top of the rue Saint-Jacques on the Rive Gauche you just had to follow a straight line. I came to love the Invalides when I accompanied my dentist friend on his trips to one of his girlfriends. She had been a successful variety singer in the 1950s and she still had the bland and restrained appeal of vinyl covers of the period. She let him get on with lukewarm enthusiasm and I passed the time by playing the aesthete, scorning the low

tables cluttered with a collection of tortoises of all sizes, in stone and in porcelain, and going to gaze through the windows at the sublime proportions of the buildings along the esplanade. Each home elicited a specific way of looking at it. In Éric's apartment, the bed was the dispatching centre of a kaleidoscope of camera lenses, screens and mirrors; in Bruno's, based on the model of Mondrian's studio, a vase of flowers was the only focal point in a space where the door jambs, the beams, the frames of the cupboards and the furniture all seemed to be one continuous unit, all with homogenous proportions, as if the same volume repeated several times served a variety of functions, as if the big dining table, for example, was merely an elevated replica of the bed.

I carry in me a sweet nostalgia for large apartments in Italian cities. When my collaboration with Enzo began he was living in Rome, in what I think was an outlying part of the city, in one of those ochre buildings separated from others by dodgy spaces. When I compared this area to the suburb of my childhood, I was amazed that there was so much fallow space. There must have been a sort of feudal urbanism dictating that each building should be able to project its entire shadow onto the ground in the evening. Inside, the rooms were much larger than those in French apartments of a comparable standard. One's voice echoed in the bathroom, and the tiling which covered the floor of the entire apartment was so clean that it made it all the easier to appreciate the full extent of the space, as if someone had just finished buffing it in honour of our visit. After a couple of years Enzo moved to Milan. The buildings were older, the apartments even more spacious, the ceilings higher. There was no more furniture. It was such

a pleasure wandering around it with nothing on, as pristine as the fresh paint on the walls, as true to myself as the bedroom, furnished with only a bed and an open suitcase! Pulling off my sweater and letting my skirt slip to the floor caused a movement of air which aroused my entire body.

On the threshold

The reader will understand more readily why I have made such an intimate connection between physical love and a mastering of space when I explain that I was born into a family of five living in a three-room apartment. And it was the first time I escaped the place that I fucked for the first time. That was not why I left, but that was what happened. Those who have been brought up in more well-off families, where each member has their own room, where individual intimacy is at least respected, or also those who have walked to school in the country may not have had the same experience. Discovering their body was not so dependent on the need to expand the space within which the body moved. Whereas I had to cover geographical distances to reach parts of myself. I had to go from Paris to Dieppe in a Renault 4 and to sleep facing the sea to learn that somewhere in a part of me that I could not see and that I had not imagined I had an opening, a cavity that was so supple and so deep that the extension of flesh that meant a boy was a boy, and I was not, could be accommodated there.

The expression has fallen into disuse, but it used to be said of a young boy or girl who was not thought to know

the process by which the human race is perpetuated, and
– by extension – not to know how love and the satisfaction of the senses are connected, that he or she was
'innocent'. I remained almost completely 'innocent' until I
had direct experience of the first act of that process. I was
twelve when my periods started. My mother and grandmother got into quite a state and called the doctor, my
father popped his head round the door and asked with a
laugh whether I had a nose bleed. So much for teaching
me the facts of life. I had no clear idea of where this blood
was coming from, and I couldn't distinguish between the
passages through which my urine and my periods passed.
One day the doctor tactfully explained to me that I should
clean myself rather more deeply than I was with my
flannel, otherwise, he said, sniffing the latex-covered
finger that had examined me, 'it doesn't smell very nice'. I
eventually suspected something because of a scandal at a
rock concert. My mother and her friends were talking
about it in front of me. The concert had caused an out-
break of violence and the police had had to intervene.
'Apparently some of the girls were so far gone that they
even took the policemen's truncheons and stuck them up
themselves!' Stuck them up where? And why exactly
would they want truncheons? Questions that unsettled me
for a long time.

I was an adolescent but remained within the ignorance
of my infantile onanism. As a very little girl I had realised
that some games afforded me exquisite and incomparable
sensations. I played with dolls in a specific and unusual
way. I would gather the crotch of my knickers into a thick
strip of fabric and wedge it into the cleft between my legs
right up to my buttocks, and I would sit down so that the

fabric dug into me slightly. In that position, I would take the tiny concave hand of a celluloid baby Ken doll and let it roam over a naked Barbie. Later, I would replace the action of the bunched knickers with rubbing together the two swollen lips at the front of the cleft. I had stopped playing with dolls, but I would picture myself in a situation similar to that of the Barbie doll, and I was entitled to the same diet of caresses. Perhaps because this activity gave me so much satisfaction, I didn't try to find out more about the ways in which a man and a woman can be together. But here is the point I wanted to make: whilst in my mind, several different boys ran their hands over my body, in reality that body remained hunched, almost paralysed, apart from the tiny toing and froing of my hand clamped in my groin. My mother had not slept with my father for several years. He had stayed in what had been their bedroom, and she had come into the second bedroom to share the double bed with me, while my brother slept in a single bed to one side. Even when you haven't been told anything, you instinctively know which activities should be kept hidden. What a paradox that I should have been forced to acquire such dexterity to give myself pleasure while barely moving or breathing so that my mother, who touched me when she turned over, wouldn't feel me quivering! The fact that I had to rely more on mental pictures than on blatant physical caresses may well have developed my imagination. Despite my best efforts, it did happen: there were times when my mother shook me and called me a dirty little girl. When I went to Dieppe with Claude, I was no longer sleeping in the same bed as my mother, but even then – and for many years – I still masturbated in a tightly hunched ball. Finally, I could

say that at the same time as opening up my body, I learned to uncurl it.

Space rarely opens up to us in one go. Even in the theatre when one more curtain needs to be raised, the process can be laborious, the heavy fabric rises slowly or, when the scene is still half hidden, the mechanism gets stuck and some occult resistance defers by a few seconds the spectator's involvement and mental participation in the action. It is well known that we attach special importance to the times of transition and the places in which they took place. The sensuous pleasure I feel in airport lounges is perhaps a distant echo of the act of emancipation I achieved when I accepted Claude's invitation to go with him, and stepped through the door with no knowledge of what the end of the journey would bring. But space is only ever an immeasurably large balloon with a hole. If you blow it up too fast, it will readily turn on you and deflate just as quickly.

I must have been thirteen or fourteen when I belatedly witnessed a 'primal scene'. As I walked along the corridor I saw my mother on the threshold of our front door with the friend who used to come and see her when my father was away. They were exchanging a slight kiss, but her eyes were closed and her back was arched. I took it badly. She took the fact that I took it badly badly. Three or four years later I first saw Claude framed in the same doorway. It was June. It was late when we arrived in Dieppe, and found a place on a campsite. We couldn't see that well to put up the tent. At the time a lot of students took amphetamines to keep them awake so that they could work through the night before an exam. Claude must have taken some so as not to get tired on the journey, and he

offered me one. Inside the tent, we didn't sleep. When he asked me quietly whether he could actually penetrate me, I was trembling. I couldn't really say if it was because of what was happening or because of what I had swallowed. In any event, I felt thoroughly unsure about my state. A few months earlier I had indulged in some heavy petting with a boy. He had put his prick onto my naked stomach and had come. The next day I had my period. My knowledge of physiology was so hazy that I thought this blood was the blood of the deflowered. Particularly as after that I waited a very long time for my next period (young girls' cycles are often irregular and can be disrupted by emotional upheavals), and I thought that I was pregnant! I told Claude that I would say yes if he asked me the question again and used my name. He can't have been expecting that sort of demand and willingly said 'Catherine' several times. When he withdrew I was scarcely aware of a fine brown thread along the top of my thigh.

The next day we hardly left the tent where there was just room for our two bodies. We lay on top of each other and rolled over, separated from the people next to us by the canvas through which a golden, sandy light filtered. There was a family in a nearby tent. I heard the wife asking irritably: 'But what the hell are they up to in there? Aren't they ever going to come out?' and the man calmly replying: 'Leave it! They're tired. They're resting.' We did manage to extract ourselves from our lair in order to have something to eat on a little terrace. I was in quite a daze. As we headed back to the tent I noticed that the beach and the campsite which was set slightly back were cut right across by a cliff perpendicular to the sea.

I don't remember exactly how my parents got me back, but it was not without drama and not for long. A few weeks later there was the episode in the garden near Lyon that I have described at the beginning of this book. A few weeks after that I went to live with Claude. The flight to Dieppe had allowed me to 'become a woman', and I had established the right to come and go as I pleased. All the same, looking back on it, our frolicking in the tent seemed like kids' games. They remind me of the way I used to hide from adults by pulling my sheet up over my head, creating the confined but vital space of a little house of my own. Succumbing to a forbidden activity in a place regulated by communal laws, poorly protected by a thin or flawed screen, by a bit of foliage, even by a wall of human accomplices, derives – at least in part – from the same playful spirit. It represents an elementary mechanism of transgression which, paradoxically, belongs less to extroversion than to introversion; you don't make an exhibition of yourself, you turn in on your intimate pleasure, pretending to ignore the fact that it might accidentally erupt in front of spectators who are not prepared for it and might even stop it.

3. Confined space

A variety of havens

My explorations of exclusive locations in the outskirts of Paris not only filled me with the euphoria of wide open spaces, but also as a corollary, that of a game of hide and seek. In an open street, a stone's throw from the Soviet Embassy, I once found refuge in the back of a Ville de Paris van, because one of the group was a municipal employee. The men came in one by one. I knelt to suck them off or lay down and curled to one side the better to present my arse to facilitate their hold. Nothing had been provided in the back of the van to soften the ridged surface of the metal floor and each jolt was quite painful. But I could have hidden there all night, not stiffened so much because of my uncomfortable position but rather dulled and lulled by the atmosphere of my unlikely haven where I curled up and sank, like in those opaque dreams, watching myself go deeper. I didn't have to move: the rear door was raised at regular intervals, the man jumped out and a new silhouette slipped in. In that creaky little vehicle I was like a motionless idol accepting the homage of a suite of followers. I was as I had imagined myself in some of my fantasies, like – for example – the one when

I'm in a concierge's room with only my arse protruding from the curtain which hides the bed offered to a long succession of men who stamp their feet and yell abuse at each other. A 2CV van is well worth a concierge's room. But I left my metal baldaquin before they had all done. Éric, who had been keeping watch, explained the following day: on the one hand, the men were in such a state of excitement that they were beginning to get aggressive, and on the other hand because the van was threatening to keel over . . .

The cabs of articulated trucks suit much better, mainly because they are equipped with a couchette. I can never catch sight of the girls waiting by the side of the road, their bodies covered in a patchwork of skimpy accessories, a balcony bra glinting above the low-cut top which doesn't quite meet the miniskirt from under which a suspender belt protrudes . . . I can never see them without thinking of the little jump they have to make on one foot to reach for the step to get up to the customer who has stopped his vehicle. I am familiar with that impulsion the body needs and the brief subsequent ascension which carries that body up to two solid blokes who greet it delicately, accustomed as they are to limit their movements in the restricted cab. My good fortune was not having to name a price or to wait out in the cold. I didn't spend much on my outfit either. I would wear just a coat or a raincoat which would fall open like a dressing-gown on the way up. Once when I was snuggled into one of these couchettes – by chance in an International Art Transport truck, one of the main transporters of art, parked near the porte D'Auteuil – I received the most elaborate caresses. On that occasion only one of the two

truckers took care of me, at great length, to the extent that – to my surprise – he kissed me on the mouth and went on fondling me after he had come. The other one watched, first by adjusting the rear-view mirror and then he turned sideways but did not touch me. It got late, we chatted; it was a very convivial situation.

Snuggling into a couchette is an experience closely identified with childhood. Jacques and I shared one in a second-class carriage on the way back from Venice during a strike, and we were trapped in a compartment with a large family. We had to get well organized. We had elected to share a couchette between the two of us, one of the ones at the top where it is the most hot and which can't be reached without undertaking the most perilous and ridiculous contortions. The parents had taken the two bottom bunks, and the children had distributed themselves as best they could amongst the three remaining ones. We then settled into one of those lazy positions in which the human race will continue to derive certain delight for a long time yet (even if that means forgetting the entire repertoire of the Kama Sutra): that is, our bodies lay closely curled in a concave arc and I warmed my buttocks against Jacques' lap. When all the night lights had been switched off, we took our trousers down and had a deep fuck. Without a word or so much as a moan disguised as a comfortable sigh, with no movement other than the imperceptible contraction of his buttocks which scarcely rolled his hips. Anyone who has been constrained to seize their pleasure in unwanted promiscuity (in a boarding school dormitory, a small family home . . .) knows what I am talking about: if you achieve your pleasure, then it will have absorbed the utter silence and

135

the near paralysis of the bodies which were its pre-conditions, and it will have been the more intense for them. Understandably, people then try to recreate this form of promiscuity in more or less artificial ways, and some try to achieve it by choosing the most unexpected and public nooks and crannies.

Listening closely to the breathing around us which suspended its various regular rhythms when the train jolted sharply, I actually felt afraid on that couchette, me who would have been perfectly indifferent to, for example, hitching up my skirt on the platform if Jacques had had the whim to ask me – I was afraid that the children would guess what we were doing. In terms of my sharing a bed with my mother, I had changed roles; yes, I was still the one succumbing to clandestine activities but I had become the adult who might feel disgust at the child's reaction. In fact, I had not forgotten the sense of decency that I had had then, one that was all the more intransigent at that age than one would think or that one values precisely because it reflects the superiority of childhood over adulthood. Put another way, I may not have minded what the adults thought of me, but I did mind what the children thought. I didn't want to put before them some-thing they should not yet know, but something serious and precious which is not revealed carelessly. Because I had relationships with men who had children, I twice very nearly gave them a far more graphic scene than my mother's sneaked kiss with her friend. The first time I spent the night with Robert in his home – in fact, the only time – I watched him wedge the door handle with the back of a chair. 'Funny, those things you see in old adventure films really work!' I thought. In the morning,

his daughter rattled the door, demanding to see her father before leaving for school. He yelled at her to go and get ready, and said he would come and see her. Which he did. In the holidays once, during siesta time Éric's son called his father from the other side of the cotton curtain which partitioned off the bedroom. Éric detached himself from my breast by leaning on an elbow, like the lid of a box pivoting on a hinge. 'Shove off,' he bellowed angrily. 'Go on, shove off and let me sleep!' Both times I took the part of the rebuffed child.

As long as there is some wind when you overtake a very large vehicle on a motorbike, there is always a precise moment when the air snatches you. This moment comes when you have reached the front of the lorry, just before you start to pull over. There is an in-draught and your torso undergoes a double twisting motion. One shoulder is thrust forwards, the other backwards, and this movement is reversed just as sharply. You are like a sail snapping in the wind. Just seconds earlier you were cleaving through the space as it opened up before you. Suddenly, that space closes in and shakes you up, molests you. I like this feeling and I can identify it in very different situations: to feel that you are right at the heart of a space that opens and closes, stretches and contracts. And in that space you are like a rubber band that has been stretched and then released, and comes back to smack the hand holding it; you are alternately the subject which seizes its environment (even if only by looking at it) and the object which is seized. So, I felt, quite unexpectedly, in a sex-shop. I liked going there with Éric. While he kept the assistant busy with his requests, which were always extremely precise because he knew exactly what had just come out,

especially videos, I would wander around the shop. The first picture I saw, whatever it might be (a girl holding her scarlet vulva open with her manicured fingers, her head in the background, slightly raised, her gaze floating above her body with the same lost expression as a patient trying to see their feet at the end of a stretcher; another one sitting back on her heels in the traditional pin-up pose holding her massive breasts in her open palms; a young man in a three-piece suit pointing his dick towards an older woman bending over her desk [she is a lawyer or ceo]; and even body-builders intended for the homosexual customers, strapped into G-strings which look minute in comparison to their bodies), any sort of picture, graphic, photographic, cinematic, be it realist or comic (a model posing in the underwear pages of a mail-order catalogue; great droplets of cum splattered outside the margins of a comic), every image I would say even at first glance makes me feel that characteristic enervation deep between my thighs. I leafed through the magazines on display, cautiously turned over the shrink-wrapped ones. Isn't it wonderful that you can be aroused so freely, in full sight and full knowledge of all the other customers doing the same thing, even though each of them behaves as if they are searching through the display stands of their local newsagent? Aren't there grounds to admire the apparent detachment you have there when contemplating pictures and objects that at home would certainly make you lose your composure? I liked to imagine myself in a mythical world where every shop offered that sort of merchandise, in amongst other goods, and where, with apparent nonchalance, you were gradually permeated by that warm feeling, absorbed in your perusal of organs reproduced in

full colour which perfectly depicted their moist surfaces, and you might shamelessly turn and show them to the person next to you. 'Excuse me, could I borrow your paper?' 'Oh, please do.' Etc. The quiet, unassuming civility which reigns in a sex-shop spread to every aspect of social life.

Going through into the back room where the peep-show is going on is like arriving late at the theatre. You are plunged into darkness, in a circular corridor lined with 'boxes'. You need coins not to tip any usherettes but to raise the screen which hides the central stage where a girl or a couple undergo a series of unbelievably slow contortions. It is so dark in the little kiosk that I have never been able to see a thing, not even the walls; which amounts to being in a void. There is, though, a faint bluish light coming from the stage, and a beam of this light settles on the base of the member that I have just taken in my mouth, so that the perceptible space around me is reduced to this section of wrinkled flesh dotted with hairs, which I swallow rhythmically. Perhaps Éric has to go to the till to change a note for some more coins. Having turned towards the window, I then don't recognise the hands which start smoothing over my exposed buttocks; I can believe that both the hands and indeed the buttocks are far, far away from me, also on the other side of the screen. Just after we go into the kiosk, we feel each other blindly, our eyes focused on the show which we talk about. We agree that the girl has a nice pussy. The guy is a bit too cutesy. Éric would really like to watch the girl and me bringing each other off. I ask whether we could meet up with her afterwards, etc. Then we are taken up in the acceleration of our own movement; the couple in the

blue light becomes less real; they are merely the distant, almost subconscious projection of the images conjured in the minds of those busying themselves in the dark. The shadow bent over my back lets out a hoarse 'twang' as it smacks more firmly against my arse.

The fantasy exchange between the show and the real action, when you fuck while watching a peep-show, is not as fluid as what happens when you watch a video or a film on television, occasionally releasing your own grip to follow the action on the screen, and using it as a pretext for changing position. While the flickering pixels blur boundaries so that the space they delineate becomes almost an extension of the space you are in, the window at a peep-show is a hiatus which substantiates the separation between the two symmetrical parts, one that can be crossed but which remains considerable. Two further points: pornographic films have a story-line which, however formulaic, hold your attention, whereas the action in a peep-show evolves very little; finally, you can watch a film continuously or spend the night in front of the television, but the bottomless kiosk has a limit which is attained when the timer runs out.

Who doesn't have somewhere amongst their memories some of those voracious kisses, those exchanges of tongues which suddenly made full use of their complement of muscles, their great length and their monstrous adhesion, exploring each other as well as the relief of their partner's entire mouth and lips? And didn't this obscene deployment happen on some doorstep, at the foot of the stairs in an apartment block or in the corner of a porch, just where the light switches are which, of course, you

hadn't used? Adolescents rarely have somewhere they can call their own, and so their carnal displays take place in semi-public places such as side doors, stairwells and landings. I have referred above to the need felt most keenly by the urban pubescent population – to establish their own intimate sphere within forbidden spaces. The sexual instinct that civilisation has made secret finds its first spontaneous expression not behind a closed bedroom door but in places we pass through, that belong to everyone and where courtesy reaches its peak of reserve: 'Good morning. Good evening. I'm so sorry. After you . . .' Etc. The number of times I have had a breast mauled by clumsy hands in the exact spot where my neighbour usually holds the door for me. Even once I had become an emancipated adult, I still sometimes displayed sufficient masochistic impatience to let myself be manhandled like a heavy bag in a tiled hallway lit by the street lights filtering while I sat on the radiator with my knees under my chin and the cast-iron tubes digging a little further into the flesh of my buttocks with every slam. As a result, shouldn't we be asking ourselves whether the taste for transgression which encourages adults to choose this sort of place, and other even more public and uncomfortable ones, to undertake the sexual act, whether this derives from some so-called 'primary' transgression, and whether their 'perversity' should not be put down to a venal immaturity?

Before I came to know the games played on the paths of the Bois de Boulogne or the track at the porte Dauphine, my outings with Henri and with Claude allowed me to continue having these surreptitious petting sessions (pretty heavy some of them) in the public spaces of

Parisian apartment blocks. At the witching hour when thieves are abroad, we disappeared into a group of buildings, looking for a friend's apartment. Even though she was an artist and she always liked to appear very relaxed, rebellious even, she was bourgeois – we're talking boulevard Exelmans here – and, on top of that, she was the girlfriend of the man who was Henri's and my 'boss'. Our aim is childish. We go and ring on the door, and beg her most sweetly to forgive us for disturbing her. The ulterior motive is that at least one of the boys will succeed in ramming his persistent prick into the depths of her little cushion of moist flesh, impregnated with the smell of sleep. But we still have to know exactly which building and on which floor the girl was sleeping. Claude, very sure of himself, volunteers to explore one of the buildings floor by floor, probably deliberately leaving Henri and myself to linger in another where our search proves fruitless. Henri is always tender in his movements, his fingers always seem slightly awkward as if he uses them more to establish things than to hold them. I am usually more forthright. Standing clamped together, we start by stroking each other's buttocks. Mine are bare under my skirt. There is not much more of him than there is of me and I like to take a man's arse in my hand, and to be able to put my arms right round him easily. I have been with tall, well-built men but I have never snubbed the seductions of small men. If a man's size is comparable to my own, and I feel an equal division of physical strength in our embraces, I experience a very particular kind of pleasure, which probably includes the desire to feminise the man in question, even a narcissistic illusion: by holding him I can experience the same pleasure he has in holding me.

I hope, later in the book, to do justice to the intoxication that overruns me when my mouth is filled by a limp member; one of the agents of this feeling is an identification of my pleasure with the man's; the more he arches his body, the more emphatically he moans, gasps or whispers encouragement, the more I feel he is exteriorising the frantic calling coming from deep within my own genitals. For now, I must concentrate on describing the scene with Henri, given that I sucked him off with what he called astonishing ardour. How did I go about it? Following the instinctual pressure of his pubis against mine, did I let myself slip to his feet, guided down the length of his body by the persistent embrace of my arms, and then, kneeling before him did I, as I usually did, rub my face, cheeks, forehead and chin over a shape that by its form and hardness always reminds me of a darning egg? The light went out. Henri joined me on the threadbare mat and we curled up together at the bottom of the stairs, facing the lift. I extricated the object that was imprisoned behind the straining fly buttons and helped it assume the shape that suits with slow, regular movements of my hand. Then, my head bent between his legs, I continued the motion with a similar toing and froing of my lips. The light came back on, suspending my progress. I felt the hammering of fear beating in my chest and ringing in my ears, its echoes reverberating as far as the pleasurable zones in my groin . . . But no sound followed the light. While we waited, I automatically kept my hand over his organ which was now too swollen to be put back where it belonged. Then, reassured, we settled more comfortably on the stairs. Some of the rules of fucking, especially if it is performed in a place that does not lend

itself to excesses, are like the rules of courtesy: the partners take it in turns to devote themselves to the other's body, temporarily keeping their own body out of reach, just like two people exchanging thanks or desultory compliments in a one-upmanship of unselfish attention. Henri's fingers triggered a motion in my cunt like the connecting rod of a train, while I sat against the front of the stairs, taking only the surrounding light into my mouth and, although I still held his member in my hand, no longer rubbed it up and down. Then I considered myself satiated, and it was my turn to close my thighs and to bury my head back between his. Our movements took up no more space than our tightly joined bodies. The light went back on again two or three times. In the intervals between it was as if the darkness were hiding us in a crevice in the walls of the well formed by the lift shaft. The blaze of light whipped my forehead to make me suck more quickly. I now don't remember whether Henri discharged by 'day' or by 'night'. Some little patting movements with the flat of the hand to straighten out clothes and tidy hair. When Claude and I spent an evening with friends and I unexpectedly had a fuck – as I had that night – out of his sight, I couldn't meet up with him again without feeling slightly awkward. I think it was probably the same for whoever was with me. Claude was waiting for us at the foot of the stairs; he pretended he had just come from another building. Henri thought he looked strangely. We gave up on the idea of finding the girl's door.

Illness, dirt

Every confined space in which the body has felt a fulfilment inversely proportional to the available space, where it has felt all the more pleasure for being constrained, awakens in us a nostalgia for the foetal state. And we never benefit from it so much as when, safe in that secret haven, organic life reassumes its rights (whatever they may be) and we can abandon ourselves to something not unlike the beginning of a regression. If you think about it, it was not for reasons of hygiene that WCs became places in which we isolate ourselves, closets in fact. Modesty is the pretext given, but the occult explanation for this modesty is neither a fear for our dignity or a wish not to embarrass others, but the freedom to experience the pleasures of defecation without any restraint, to inhale our own embalming stench or even to examine our stools meticulously, taking a lead from Salvador Dali who left descriptions rich with comparisons and images. I am not about to tell a series of scatological stories, I just want to remember here some banal situations in which my different bodily functions found themselves in conflict. And as I have never come across any declared enthusiasts for my farts or my faeces, and I myself have had no more inclination to savour those of others, these confrontations turned out to be dubious struggles between pleasure and displeasure, enjoyment and pain.

I suffer from migraines. Having landed in Casablanca, I suffocate in the heat at the airport as I wait for ages for my luggage to come through. The journey is not yet: Basile, the architect friend who invited me, drives me to the holiday village he has built where he has a small

house. We stop off on a track away from the road. It is the most beautiful day, the sparse leaves flutter in the bright light around us. Squatting on all fours on the back seat of the car, I am, as usual, so good at sticking my arse out that I can almost imagine it as a balloon popping out of the car, ready to detach itself from the rest of my body and fly away. While this balloon is being pierced by one of the sharpest pricks I have ever known, I can feel the first symptoms. My vision is blurred by sort of flashes which accentuate the fluttering effect of the light. By the final charge, my body – with the exception of my arse – has ceased to exist, emptied of its substance like a piece of fruit left to shrivel, crumbling in the glimmering light. Or, to be more precise, there is nothing left between my head which has been turned to stone by the vice-like grip of pain, and the skin on my buttocks where the last few caresses linger. I could no longer utter a single word. When we arrived at our destination, I went and lay flat out on the deep, tall bed. Added to these two terminals to which my body was reduced (the one overwhelmed by pain, the other abandoned to lethargy by pleasure) there was now the weight of nausea which comes with very bad headaches. Now I just had the outward appearance of a body, anchored in three places by the only three organs left to me, and fussed over silently by an anxious man. When a migraine pins me in the depths of a darkened room like this, when I don't even have the strength to peel off the sheet impregnated with the sweat of a night and a day, and when breathing the dissipated stench of my own vomit is the only perception left to me which does not cause intolerable pain, my last mental resources can end up imagining strangers watching me in that state (with the

cavities around my eyes enlarged by rings of grey and the angle between the inner edge of my eyelids and the root of the nose pinched tightly together). Jacques is too accustomed to it and doctors have too much clinical distance. I would like Jacques to take photographs of me at times like that, and for them to be published and seen by people who read my books and articles, for example. When I am rendered completely powerless by such intense suffering there would be some sense of compensation in closing the circle on my physical degeneration by inscribing it on the gaze of others. My relationship with Basile has always been light and playful, and the pleasure unadulterated. If I had to be ill in front of him, then I would have to do it with the same simplicity with which I surrendered myself when he took me from behind after a good meal and I let my bulging tummy express a few farts. He was a sharp, astute man, and conversation with him was always stimulating, and one fine day he was kind enough to compliment me on the big nose which I had always had a complex about, but which he told me gave character to my face. He was also someone who usually came in my arse but not before having used a firm index finger to stimulate the most highly reactive point on my body. While I was no longer capable of exchanging a single word with him, or to respond to the touch of his hand, I could still offer him the spectacle of myself indulging in the complete negation of my being.

It is often extremely difficult to identify the cause of a headache; anyone who is prone to them will know this, and in some ways this dispenses them of any feelings of guilt when the cause is obvious and it is their fault: abuse of alcohol or too much sun. I haven't been drunk more

than two or three times in my life. On one of these occasions I was with Lucien who had slumped on top of me on the sitting room carpet, in front of his friends and unbeknown to his wife. He had taken me for dinner with a young couple who lived outside Paris. Without realising it I drank too much champagne. The couple lived in a big bungalow in which you walked straight into the kitchen which also served as a dining room. At the back of the room there were two doors next to each other, each leading to a bedroom. The evening must initially have started in their bedroom. I am trying to piece it together: Lucien takes me over onto the bed with help from the other man; they start touching me up, I undertake an investigation of their files. The young woman hangs back a bit, her friend takes her by the shoulders, kisses her, encourages her to come and lie down with us. She goes into the bathroom, he follows her and comes back explaining that 'this isn't Christine's thing, but we can do what we like, it doesn't bother her'. I partake in the goings on in the same way that I involuntarily follow a radio play echoing through the courtyard of my apartment building on a summer's day. Probably out of respect for Christine, even though she doesn't reappear – is she busying herself in front of the bathroom mirror or sitting indecisively on the side of the bath? – we move to the other bedroom.

I really can't remember whether our host penetrated me, on the other hand I do know that I apathetically let Lucien have me. The eiderdown was a deep chasm, and my tummy sank deeper into it. My vagina, worked on smoothly by Lucien (who must have realised I wasn't feeling well), softened and sank, drawn into that great depth, while a paralysing force kept my head, neck, shoulders

and even my partially spread arms flat on the bed. I did somehow find the strength to get up. How many times in the night? Four, five times? I crossed the kitchen naked, and went into the garden. It was pouring with rain. I stood and vomited straight onto the ground in the middle of the alley, not looking for somewhere to hide. It has to be said that each spasm converted the blacksmith's hammering inside my skull into something that felt like a final disintegration of the beaten piece of metal. The whole body flows into the mass of the head and forms a fist tightly grasping a lacerating blade. The cold rain momentarily appeased the pain. On my way back to the bedroom, I rinsed my mouth out in the kitchen sink. The following morning, when the life-saving medicine had been brought from the chemist, when it was all over, Lucien assured me that he had fucked me several times during the night and that I had seemed to enjoy it. It is one of the rare situations when I was not conscious of what I was doing. A few months later the young woman came to see me. She and her boyfriend had had a terrible car crash. He had died and his family had turned her out of the house they had lived in together. I felt genuine compassion for her while at the same time having a strange feeling that this was just the continuation of a nightmare.

Putting all these episodes together reminds me of another. After a not very good meal, as had been the case with Basile, it was on a day when, on the contrary, I might have eaten something that wasn't very fresh, and I had an upset stomach, Lucien absolutely insisted on taking me from behind. However hard I tried to avoid this and to distract him with a fervent fellation, I couldn't stop him delving his fingers right up close to the part of me that was

sick, and I realised to my shame that they brought out a small amount of liquid matter. He buried his dick in there. The pleasure that this particular use of the rectum gives is obviously in the same family as that experienced in the seconds before the expulsion of faecal matter, but in this case the conjugation of the two was so narrow that it bordered on torture. I have never taken part in scatological games, either of my own free will or encouraged by a man with that sort of experience. I have noticed that if and when these sort of incidents occurred at all it was with men much older than myself, both of whom could be deemed – although both for different reasons – father figures. When he withdrew, Lucien went to wash himself with no other commentary than to say that I had been silly to make such a fuss because it had been so good. I felt I could trust him.

There is such a perfect feeling of well-being when you have, so to speak, left your body behind in accesses of pleasure with someone else, but you can recognise some aspects of that well-being when you leave your body behind in the opposite circumstances, in abjection or even the most intense pain. I have dealt with the theme of the open space we appropriate for ourselves, and of our temptation to let strangers look on our nudity like at a shop window. In these instances, we actually wear our nudity like a garment, and displaying it relates to the same sort of excitement we feel when, conversely, we prepare our bodies, dress them and put on our make-up to seduce. I emphasise the word excitement, the rising tide of desire waiting for a response from the outside world. It surely cannot be excitement that we feel when we recoil into the closed world of pain or in the immediate satisfaction of

elementary functions: when the body doesn't have the strength to occupy any other space than the sunken outline carved into a mattress, when the spew of vomit splatters the feet, when a dribble of shit trickles between our thighs. If there is any pleasure in this, it is not that the body feels struck by something greater than itself, it is that it feels bottomless, as if by exteriorising the activities of our entrails we could accede to our entire surroundings.

If one of the meanings of the word 'space' is emptiness, if when it is used without any qualification it principally evokes a clear sky or a desert, a confined space is seen almost as automatically as a filled space. When I feel the need to return my aspirations to vast horizons, I happily transport myself to a dustbin site, usually the one at the foot of the building in which I grew up. Back to the wall, I am shafted between the corrugated surfaces of the bins by a man who by necessity puts down his bucket of garbage. I have never enacted this fantasy but I assiduously maintained a relationship with a man who lived in such a shambles and so much filth that a platonic dustbin must have had a place somewhere in his unconscious. This same man was an aesthete, a clear and precise theoretician with a rather precious turn of phrase. His apartment consisted of two minute rooms whose walls were completely covered in shelves laden with books and records, distributed at random, and some had given way under their weight. Three quarters of one of the rooms was taken up with the bed where I had only ever seen the top sheet and the blanket scuffed up in a heap, and which you could only get into after pushing aside books, papers and newspapers. In the second room it was

not only the desk which looked as if it had suffered the revenge of a burglar furious not to have found what he was looking for, but also the floor; it was covered with a maze of crumbling piles of books and catalogues, heaps of opened envelopes and crumpled paper, fanned out sheaves of paper which one might think still of some use. This along with the dust would have been nothing if it hadn't been for the glasses with the dried brown mark of long-forgotten drinks used as paperweights, if they hadn't left their slimy circular imprint on other pieces of paper, if a greyish T-shirt or a stiffened face towel hadn't been jumbled into the bed sheets, if – when you wanted to locate a bar of soap in the sink – you didn't have to search through archaeological layers of cups and saucers encrusted with crumbs, like the mud still attached to recently exhumed relics . . . all of that made you heave. I spent many nights in this hovel. The occupier seemed not to notice. The fact that he never accomplished that elementary act of comfort – brushing his teeth – I found strange. When he laughed, his upper lip raised the curtain on a yellow plaster dotted with black patches. As I was sure that all mothers taught their children this hygienic routine, I wondered exactly what level of amnesia he had achieved on the subject of his childhood. He liked to be finger-fucked up his arse. From the outset he would put himself on all fours, presenting his large rather white bottom, and his face serious while he waited. Then I would kneel squarely beside him with my left hand resting gently on his back or his hip, and my moistened right hand would start by rubbing round the outside of his anus, then I would put in two fingers, three, four. With my back bent and my frenetic arm movements I must have

looked very like a housewife desperately trying to stop a sauce curdling, or someone proudly polishing up their DIY achievement. His moans had the same nasal resonance as his laugh. Measuring the fruits of my sustained efforts by listening to them afforded me such an extreme state of excitement that it was only with great regret that I abandoned the movement which had become painful. Then we undertook a series of positions, with the logic of acrobats who end up exchanging places as they flow from one movement to the next. I would substitute my tongue for my fingers, then I would slide underneath him to perform what is called a sixty-nine, then it would be my turn to go on all fours. The acute level of pleasure that I then reached was also a recurring subject for interrogation. Not many people knew his lair, and wallowing in it undoubtedly revived the childish predilection for sewers. Sewers are hidden places, not so much because it would be humiliating to be seen there but because, following the example of animals that release a powerful stench to put off a predator, we hide ourselves in them like a protective envelope, we take refuge in them like a nest that is all the more secure for being partly strewn with our own excretions. Even so, my friends were in a position to confirm that the man in question was dirtier than is usually acceptable for intellectuals who often neglect their physical appearance. I didn't discourage their questions or their comments. There was a controlled defiance in my response: 'Well, yes, I go just as I am now – freshly showered and in clean knickers – and rub myself up against that filth.' Or if need be: 'I rub myself against him just like I'm cuddling up to you.'

You don't have to be a great psychologist to deduce

from this behaviour an inclination for self-abasement, mixed with the perverse intention of taking the other. But this tendency doesn't stop there; I was carried by the conviction that I rejoiced in extraordinary freedom. To fuck above and beyond any sense of disgust was not just a way of lowering oneself, it was, in a diametrically opposite move, to raise yourself above all prejudice. There are those who break taboos as powerful as incest. I settled for not having to choose my partners, however many of them there may have been (given the conditions under which I gave myself, if my father had happened to be one of the 'number', I would not have recognised him), and I can also say whatever sex they may have been and whatever their physical and moral qualities may have been (in the same way that I have never tried to avoid a man who didn't wash, I have with full knowledge had sexual contact with three or four who were completely spineless and stupid). And I was still waiting to find myself under a trained dog, as Éric kept promising, but it never happened, either because the opportunity just didn't arise or because he thought it ought to stay in the realms of fantasy. Earlier on in this book, I applied my thoughts to the theme of space. I have now just spoken of animals and of immersing oneself into human bestiality. What path should I take to convey most clearly the contrasting experiences of pleasure which projects us outside ourselves and filth which belittles us? Perhaps this one: On some plane journeys I like looking out over desert landscapes. Being shut up in the cabin on a long-haul flight promotes a general sloppiness amongst the passengers and, in that promiscuity, you end up exchanging the smells of musty armpits and overheated feet with those

sitting next to you. The feeling of wonderment I have if I have an opportunity to look over a stretch of Siberia or the Gobi desert is all the greater if I am shackled not so much by my seat belt as by the soupy bath in which I am submerged.

In the office

I feel a need to suture the cut between the interior and the exterior of my body, and, without going so far as a frank anality, a facility for finding appeasement in filth: some of the traits of my sexual personality support slight regressive tendencies. I would add to that my habit of completing the sexual act in a maximum number of places of my familiar space. Some of these places allow a couple to express the urgency of their desire and, at the same time, to experiment with unusual positions, between the lift and the door to the apartment, in the bath or on the kitchen table. Some of the most exciting locations are in the work place. Here intimate space and public space meet. One friend whom I used to meet in his office over-looking the rue de Rennes, would happily let himself be sucked off in front of the floor to ceiling window, and the euphoric activity in that part of Paris which bubbled up to me from the street as I knelt silhouetted against this window must have contributed to my pleasure. In cities, deprived of distant horizons, I like being able to look out from a window or balcony while I keep a languorous dick captive in a secret place. At home, my gaze roams over the narrow courtyard and the neighbour's windows; from an office I once worked in on the boulevard Saint-Germain I

contemplated the vast facade of the Ministry of Foreign Affairs. I have also mentioned some of these places when I spoke of the exquisite fear of exposing oneself to involuntary witnesses. To this exhibitionist temptation, I could add the impulse to mark one's territory as an animal would. Like a lemur which marks out its chosen space with a few jets of urine, you leave a few drops of cum on a staircase or the office carpet, you impregnate the storeroom where everyone hangs up their coats. By inscribing this terrain with the act in which a body exceeds its limits, you appropriate it for yourself by osmosis. And you take it from others. There is without doubt a degree of provocation or even of indirect aggression towards others in this operation. Our freedom seems all the greater when we claim it in a place where professional cohabitation usually imposes rules and limitations, even if you share that place with the most discreet and tolerant people. Not to mention the fact that we can to some extent embroil them without their knowledge by annexing their belongings into our most private spheres: a sweater they forgot which you park your buttocks on, or the hand towel in the office toilets which you use to wipe between your legs. There are some places that I have occupied in this way, and I have felt more at home in them than those who spent the best part of their active time there, because I had left the damp outline of my buttocks in the place devoted to their work and their files. This didn't stop me from entertaining the idea that they too might have subverted the role of their work space, and that we were fucking in each other's wake.

I have methodically laid out the markers of a sexual territory within a professional location. Some places lend themselves particularly well, such as a photographic dark-

room or those windowless store-rooms in which parcels of newspapers are usually kept. The first is closed off by a blackout curtain. It is so small that you have to stay standing, bathed in cabaret-like light. This light makes the skin look soft as velvet, and this optical impression exacerbates the touch; you only need to brush your hands lightly over each other. Especially as you feel disembodied: the red light makes pale skin almost transparent, and swallows up the darker areas, hair or one's clothes.

In a store-room the most unsettling thing is choosing a place. The area carved up into parallel alleys by the shelving is perfectly uniform, you are no less sheltered from intruders in one alley than another, and you would anyway be seen through the blank spaces between the piles of paper. The net result is that you settle in this place of accumulation as arbitrarily as you would in an empty space, and not before you have turned and looked about you a few times. In this sort of place fellatio was preferable for me as the act that was easiest to interrupt. I think that it was to do with the gloominess of the place. In a wood, on a deserted track, in any sort of public place, there is always a good reason to choose to hide behind this clump of trees or in that doorway, either because it offers the greatest comfort or safety, or because it has some playful or aesthetic quality. But here there was none of that. So your stop here was necessarily brief because you could just as easily move a few metres away, and migrate from place to place. I would add to that the fact that, if we are happy to contemplate being caught *in flagrante delicto* in a picturesque setting, there would be something almost humiliating about being caught in somewhere as ugly as that.

I like the atmosphere of a deserted office, there is a feeling of calm which does not represent an end of activity, merely a suspension of it. The harassment of the working day is over, but it still threatens in the shape of a telephone ringing persistently, the gaping jaw of a computer monitor, a file left open. All the tools, all the materials and all the space at my disposal – and mine alone – give me the illusory but calming impression that I have an unlimited capacity for work. As I have already said, when others vacate space, they also vacate time, and it is as if I have all eternity at my disposal to learn how to use every piece of equipment, and to analyse and resolve every problem; it is as if the very fact that I can go into an office without having to introduce myself or apologise smoothes out my fitful, halting life. In these situations, and when I was joined in my solitary pursuit by a colleague who doubled as a sexual partner, I only very occasionally made use of the relative comfort of the carpet. Worktops were more commonly my platforms. You might think it was because that position, with the woman sitting on the edge of a table and the man standing between her legs, is easier to modify if a colleague should burst into the room. This is not so. It was actually because the movements flowed naturally. Vincent used to make up the dummies, and he and I would sometimes stand side by side looking through the page layouts, not thinking to sit down because he was a man in a hurry and perhaps because we felt we could evaluate them better with an extra 30cm distance. The slightest hesitation in the team of our work and I would turn round. One quick hop and, with my buttocks next to the dummies, my pubis was at the right level. And the level matters. Quite often the best moment to slip from a

professional discussion to a silent embrace corresponds to a lapse in concentration, when, for example, you need to look for a document in a bottom drawer. As I bend over to get it, I push out my buttocks. All they want is to be grasped by two firm hands. Then they need a desk to lean on; I am always very cautious if I have to clear everything aside to lie on my back. But not all work surfaces are at the correct height, many are too low, and there are some desks I never went back to a second time. One graphic designer I used to go to see at his agency had cleverly addressed the problem by acquiring pedestal chairs whose height can be adjusted to the nearest centimetre. I would sit down on it in front of him, my genitals exactly opposite his. We had arranged to have a table behind him for me to put my feet on. We could stay like that for a long time without either of us tiring, for me it was like lying in a deck chair, while he rolled his supple waist as if he were turning a hula hoop. Intermittently he would substitute his own movement with that of the chair seat, grabbing it with both hands and swinging it fluidly from side to side.

Taboos

I have rarely worried about being caught fucking *in flagrante*. In the above pages, I have referred several times to the awareness of risk there is if you undertake a sexual occupation in a place not intended for that purpose, because this awareness also contributes to the pleasure. Even so, the risk is almost always calculated, limited by implicit conventions: someone used to the Bois could draw a map of the places that are out of bounds but where

the act is nevertheless possible and those where it would definitively be impossible, and I have hardly ever made use of offices except outside working hours . . . In a rather prosaic way the conviction that sexuality, in whatever form it may take, is the most widely shared thing in the world reassures me that nothing unpleasant will happen. An involuntary witness to a sexual act (if he is not driven to join in) would still be sufficiently confused by his own impulses to show no reaction, to maintain a discreet reserve. Jacques who, with a smile, worries about what would have happened if the young back packer who has just greeted us had passed us two minutes earlier – when, that is, we had our trouser belts round our ankles, and our bucking bodies rustled the leaves by the side of the path, making exactly the same noise as some little animal running for cover, I say nothing would have happened.

I would add to that that I fear only those that I know too well, not the anonymous who mean nothing to me, and I don't think I am alone in this. In this area, the taboo for me would be to use the home that you share with someone else, while that person was out and unaware of what was going on. Early one afternoon Claude came home to the apartment – a big bourgeois apartment we had just moved into – and into the spare bedroom near the front door. He interrupted a copulation I had not been able to resist. It was the first time that, not in a group session, I had had the full benefit of Paul's large body, which crushed me most pleasurably. Claude went back out without a word. I saw Paul stand up, his back filling the door frame, his naked buttocks proportionately so small as he followed Claude. Through the door I heard him say: 'I'm sorry, old man.' I was struck by the

unaffected tone he used to express his genuine discomfort. I, on the other hand, even though I had already fucked Paul in front of Claude, and even though Claude never referred to the incident, couldn't think about it without feeling persistent guilt for a very long time. At least I could see the spare room as relatively neutral territory. Our shared bedroom, the 'conjugal' bed was absolutely out of bounds. On one occasion the deliquescence of my entire body and of my will (which I have already mentioned, as I have my fatal reaction to a man's first touch) led me to the threshold of that room, the room that is still ours, Jacques' and mine. But I found I couldn't even lean against the door frame, unconsciously afraid that I would release the spring of a trap. So I had to hop backwards because the man kneeling in front of me and trying to get to the mound under my skirt had automatically put one of my legs over his shoulder. I lost my balance at the foot of the bed. His incredulous face stared at me through the V of my upturned legs. I brought an end to the exercise and got back to my feet aloofly.

These are the limits set by a morality which belongs more to the realms of superstition than to a clear understanding of what would be right and what would be wrong. Firstly, these limits or markers only send signals in one direction; I have never had any scruples in someone else's bathroom about using her perfumed soap to chase away the fetid residue of the night. Then, I may have cheated on someone in a way which, if and when it was revealed, might have hurt him much more than to find out that I had cavorted in his sheets with someone else. I appropriate to other people the same adherence to environment that I have myself, which makes every

intimate thing – or any thing that has served an intimate purpose – a sort of extension of the body, a sensitive prosthesis. If, while someone is away, you touch something that they are close to, they themselves are involved by contiguity. During an orgy, my tongue could easily lick round a pussy which had just been stuffed by a man who had first got off on me, but the thought of drying myself on a towel that some woman who came clandestinely to my home may have used to wipe between her thighs, or the thought that Jacques might use the same one as some guest of mine whose visit he knew nothing about, horrifies me as much as an epidemic of leprosy. What is more, as a precursor to this fear itself, a hierarchy is established in my mind, granting greater importance to a respect for physical integrity (everything attached to it and that I attach to it . . .) than for moral serenity; because I consider that it is more irremediable to damage the first than the second. Although I have managed to relativise this theory, I tend to think that we 'cope' better with an invisible wound than an external wound. I am a formalist.

Trusting

There is a paradox with respect to this character trait and that is that, even though images have such a dominant role in my life and even though my eye guides me far more than any other organ, during the sexual act it is as if I am blind. You could say that within the continuum of the world of sex, I move like a cell within its tissue. The nocturnal outings, and the fact of being surrounded, carried and penetrated by shadows suit me well. Better

still, I can follow my partner blindly. I put myself in his hands, abandoning my free will; his presence stops anything nasty happening to me. When I was with Éric we could drive for ages towards some destination unknown to me – I could end up in open country or level-3 in an underground car park, I never asked any questions. When all was said and done whatever happened was less strange than nothing happening at all. I have bad memories of the basement of a Moroccan restaurant, near the place Maubert, not an area we often went to. There were couches and low tables under the vault where it was chilly. We had dined there alone, me with my breasts bared and my skirt hitched right up. Each time the waiter or the man that I thought was the owner brought dishes over, Éric would push my top a bit further aside and run his hand insistently under my skirt. I remember less about the heavy and not altogether friendly way these two men looked at me, than I do about the way they touched me, quickly, sporadically, on my companion's tacit invitation. It was I who brought the waiting to an end by burying Éric's organ in my mouth. Surely my intention was to escape from the less than friendly attentions of the staff? We left the restaurant without finishing our meal. Were the usual customers not there? Did Éric know the place well, and hadn't he overestimated the welcome we might be granted? I felt more apprehensive than if I had been in some incongruous place and a herd of strangers had set upon me with their dicks hanging out. With Éric I always knew that anyone we met, in whatever circumstances, could, on some imperceptible sign from him, open my thighs and slip in his member. I didn't think there could be any exceptions to this, as if Éric has been a sort of

universal ferryman, not to take me across to some promised land, but in order to let people penetrate me, one after another. Hence my uneasiness that evening.

In the undefined places where I met people whose diverse social backgrounds were levelled by a sexual egalitarianism, I was never confronted with any threats or violence, I was even gratified with a degree of attention that I didn't always find in a classic two-person relationship . . . As for any fear of the police, there was no such thing. On the one hand, I have a childlike trust in the ability of the man I am with, to ensure our safety – and, in fact, there was never a single incident. On the other, even though I feel overcome with shame when a conductor asks me rather rudely for a ticket I have temporarily lost, I would only have been put out if I had been caught in the act exhibiting myself on the public highway. The body discovered by the representative of the law would have been no more or less than the body penetrated by the stranger in the Bois, not so much an inhabited body as a shell from which I had withdrawn. This reckless lack of concern is also at the root of the determination and perseverance I can display during the act, and – indeed – other activities, and which is not unrelated to the dissociation that I have just mentioned: either the conscience is annihilated by that determination and can no longer view the act with any distance, or, quite the opposite, when the body is surrendered to automatic functions, the conscience escapes and loses any association with that act. At times like that, no external factor can disturb my body or my partner's, because nothing exists outside the space they occupy. And how small that space is! You rarely fuck expansively in a

public place. You tend instead to burrow into each other.

There are few places that have as many forbidden areas as a museum: the works themselves are roped off, and there are plenty of places from which the public are banned. The visitor makes his progress with a vague sense that there is another parallel world, which he cannot see but from which he is being watched. Henri, myself and a friend called Fred therefore took advantage of a door that had exceptionally been left ajar at the end of a vast, momentarily deserted gallery in the Museum of Modern Art in Paris. We slipped in behind a flimsy partition wall which hid the pandemonium of what I imagine was a temporary store-room. We didn't go far into the room. It was very cluttered; but more particularly we made our minds up quickly, without thinking it over. Still, I could see the shaft of light on the floor, because we had left the door as it was, while I formed a bridge between the two men. After a few minutes they changed places. They both came, one in my cunt, the other in my mouth. I don't know which one of them intermittently suspended the action of his prick to run his hand under my stomach and pleasure me. It encouraged me to do it myself and to set off my own orgasm while the shrinking prick still lingered in my cunt and the other, whose cum I had swallowed, had moved away to free me from one of my moorings the better to enjoy my pleasure. This led to a little conversation about the way I masturbated. I explained, believing that I was revealing something astonishing, that in less precarious circumstances I could have had two or three consecutive orgasms. They made fun of me. That was very common for a woman, they claimed, as we slowly tucked our shirts back into our trousers. When we went back out

into the light, the museum was just as empty. We carried on looking round the exhibition. I went from one painting to another, and from Henri to Fred for their comments, and this visit was all the more enjoyable because it was bolstered by the complicity which from then on would link me to those two men and to that place.

In that dark store-room, with my body bent double between two other bodies and my eyes staring vertically down, I was well hemmed in. I am convinced that when my field of vision is limited then, in some primitive way, this conjures up anything that could threaten me or simply upset me, in fact anything that I don't want to countenance for one reason or another. The body of whoever I am with becomes an obstacle, and whatever lies beyond it that I cannot see doesn't really exist. So, in the position I was in at the museum, only this time on the first floor of a shop selling sadomasochist gear on the boulevard de Clichy – again in a stock-room – I have one cheek pressed up against Éric's stomach while he held me by my shoulders and the owner of the boutique rams my rear end onto his dick. Before assuming this position, I notice that the man is very small and thick-set with short arms, but as soon as he disappears from view his person disintegrates. So much so that I speak to Éric and not directly to him to ask him to put a condom on before penetrating. He is perturbed by this request and forced to rummage through some boxes; he admits quietly that he is afraid his wife might come in. Even though he has a thick organ that has to force entry, he hovers in limbo the whole time. A girl who looks like a shy employee watches the whole scene rather sullenly. From time to time, I catch her eye, as I glance sideways; her eyes are black, probably

ringed with kohl. I feel as if I am on a stage, separated by some indistinct void from a gloomy spectator waiting for the action to start. When I look at her I am in some ways looking back at myself, and I end up seeing myself, but just the head, the neck hunched back into my shoulders, the cheek crushed against Éric's jacket and scuffed by the zip, the mouth is open, whereas what is going on above the waist is part of a sort of back-drop. The midget's pokes become as unreal to me as a thundering sound heard from the wings to imply some far-off action.

Another time, in a sauna, it was the friendliness of a little masseuse which brought about this duality. The tiers of slatted wooden benches had forced me to keep turning round. I had alternately bent and reached up to take all the eager pricks in my mouth. I don't sweat much. So I stayed dry long enough for each of them to grab hold of me while I myself had to make great efforts to hold on to and direct pieces of flesh which had become viscous and slippery. All the way to the showers, my clitoris had been aggressed and my nipples pinched. Eventually I lay down aching on the massage table. The girl spoke softly, leaving a pause between her sentences in the same way that she stopped to put talc on her hands between each series of movements. She was sympathising with my fatigue. When you feel like that, there's nothing quite like a steam bath followed by a good massage, is there! She feigned ignorance of exactly what sort of ordeals I had just subjected my body to, and she spoke to me as a beautician would, offering professional but also maternal ministrations to a modern active woman who without reserve puts herself into her hands. I have always liked slipping into a role, especially in this sort of situation, and

I replied to her questions, relaxing more by this con-
formism than by the action of her fingers. It amused me to
feel her kneading muscles which a few moments earlier
had been subjected to more carnal pressures. She also
seemed distant. I was separated from her by a succession
of transformations. She took on a disguise constructed by
the course of our conversation, but beneath this disguise
was my skin, which she touched so gently, overlaying the
other caresses that had gone before, and I abandoned this
skin to her just as willingly, like a cast-off. After all, I was
no more the debauched little bourgeoise she must have
taken me for than the steadfast one we were inventing.
As far as I know we were the only two women in the
establishment that evening, but I thought of myself as
being in the active realm of the men – and, in a way, they
were still standing round me – whereas I saw her in a
passive feminine realm, a place she occupied as an
observer, and the two were incontrovertibly separate.

In the end, the selection operated by my sight is intensified by the assured protection of my partner's gaze,
by the veil with which he covers me, a veil which is of
course both opaque and transparent. Jacques does not
tend to choose the busiest places to take pictures of me
naked – he would only exhibit me in a photo – but he has
a predilection for places one passes through, and more
particularly for the transitory nature of the things you find
in them (the wrecks of abandoned cars, pieces of
furniture, ruins . . .), which took us to the places where
these things are used. We are cautious. I always wear a
dress that is easy to button back up again. In the frontier
station of Port-Bou, we wait until the platform is empty.
There is a train pulling out, but it is two or three

platforms away. Anyway, the people are far too busy to notice us, and we make sure that the three or four frontier guards are still chatting to each other. I am looking into the light so I can't really make out the signs Jacques is giving me. I start walking towards him with the dress open right down the front. I gain confidence as I go. Hypnotised by the fluttering of the silhouette waiting for me at the far end, I feel as if I am carving out my own channel as I go, opening up the acrid, laden air to form a space no wider than the gap between my two swinging arms. Each click of the camera confirms the impunity of my advance. When I reach the end, I lean against the wall. Jacques takes a few more pictures. More nonchalance is authorised once the open space is behind me. The euphoria of a conquest: we were no more interrupted in the underpass which links the platforms to each other, or in the large, empty, echoing concourse, or on the little terrace invaded by cats and graced with a fountain which one of the station entrances opened out onto.

The second photographic session of the day takes place in the sailors' cemetery, in the walkways between the rows of family graves built in several storeys, on Benjamin's tomb, in a game of hide-and-seek with two or three slow walking women. It seems obvious to me to be naked in the sea air and amongst the dead. But I feel unsure about being in so ambiguous a place, both open to all and profoundly private, standing between the horizon and the framing lens. It is not the balustrade which holds me safe above the drop, but his gaze on me, alternately driving me on and following me, and unfurling between us like an anchor. When I face the sea and turn my back on the camera so that I am no longer aware of how far it is from

me, then the lens seems to attach itself to my shoulders and the small of my back, drawing me in with a powerful suction.

After supper, we go back to the car which is parked near the cemetery. Now we make the most of the evening light for a little rubbing up, croup to flies. My undressing requires that we up the stakes; having done nothing but unbutton and undress, I want to open myself up wide again. I am half lying on the bonnet and my cunt is getting ready to swallow the end of his prick when the air is sliced by violent barking. A little dog crosses the halo of light around the only street lamp, a man hobbles along behind him. Brief moment of confusion: I push the skirt of my dress back down, Jacques manages as best he can to stow his now unpliable parts. Still stroking him through the thickness of his trousers, I insist that we watch which way the man goes who, as if this was meant to happen, is now pacing up and down watching us out of the corner of his eye. Jacques decides it would be better to go home. In the car, in the state of panic I always have when I am very frustrated, I am overcome with anger. I counter Jacques' cautious comments by saying the man might have come and joined us. Exasperated desire is a naive dictator which cannot believe anyone would oppose it or even inconvenience it. Isn't it also that I feel I have been abandoned by the extreme attentiveness which has followed me and protected me all day and which was to some extent my link with the world? Anger derives from a sense of powerlessness. When my need to be penetrated is thwarted, I am torn between these two conflicting states: on the one hand an incredulity which means I cannot understand the reasons (however reasonable they

may be) why my partners aren't responding to my imperious waiting; and on the other hand, an equally stupid inability to break down their resistance (however circumstantial, definitive or wavering it may be), in other words to take the initiative by making some seductive or provocative gesture which would make them change their minds. I wait stubbornly, exhaustingly, for some initiative on the other's part which they may never take. How many times have I resented Jacques when this urge came to me while doing something quite ordinary, some domestic chore for example, but I didn't let it show and I somehow felt reproachful towards him for failing to read the circumvolutions of my brain where the source of my libido lies? If I can be forgiven for drawing a parallel with a situation that bears no comparison with these capricious outbursts of mine, I would compare it to the state of someone who, since birth or as a result of an accident, doesn't have the use of their limbs or the power of speech, but whose intelligence and need to communicate remain intact. They depend entirely on those around them to break through their isolation. It is said that this entourage of theirs can have some degree of success if they pay minute attention to the subtlest signals, such as blinking, from the patient, or by massaging them patiently to awaken their nerve endings. Sexual frustration plunges me into what I would call a benign autism which makes me utterly dependant on a twinkle of lust in someone else's eye and the caresses they have the goodness to offer. On that condition, my anxiety dissipates and I can reclaim my place in an environment that is no longer hostile to me.

On the way home, I ask to stop on the road side. But my anger only increases because we are on a red route and

it really wouldn't be possible. So I cut myself off from the road and the car. I concentrate all my attention on my pubis which I thrust forwards and I become absorbed in a slow circular stroking movement of that sort of sticky little animal that lives there. From time to time the headlights of oncoming cars light up my stomach as smooth as porcelain. What sort of mirage am I burying myself in then? Surely not a continuation of the events which were left in suspense a few minutes earlier. That particular business is over. No, I prefer taking refuge in one of my reassuring old scenarios, a long way away from where I really am. In an intense, sustained effort of concentration, I construct the scene in great detail, perhaps the one in which I am pulled to pieces by countless fingering hands on a stretch of wasteland or in the toilets of a fleapit cinema – I don't really remember. When Jacques stretches out his arm, without taking his eyes off the road, and traces blind, sweeping movements over my breasts and stomach, and when he dives his hand down to fight mine and gain possession of its soaking toy, he upsets the smooth running of the scene. I resist the urge to stop him.

As we come into Perpignan, Jacques parks the car on a brightly lit, empty car park at the foot of a tower block. In order to get close to me and because of the gap between the seats, he has to throw his chest forward like a gargoyle. His head comes into my field of vision and eclipses everything. He brings me off with three or four vigorous fingers. I like hearing the smacking sound of my wet labia; the frankness of this noise wakes me from my fantasies. I never stretch out my body to offer it up to these caresses straight away or that easily. Before I give in and spread my thighs wide, before I throw my head back

and open up my arms to offer up my breasts, I need a little time. Time, perhaps, to uncoil from the curled position I automatically assumed, a position imprinted on my body when, as a child, I had to hide my masturbating; time to accept – as usual and once again (and even after manoeuvring in front of a camera for hours) – to show my body all at one in its entirety. It is not nudity that I am afraid of – quite the contrary – it is the snapshot moment of revelation. And it is even less because I hesitate to abandon myself to others – absolutely the contrary! – it is that I don't know how to move from my introspective vision to seeing myself. In fact, to achieve it I need the other's gaze. I can't say: 'There, look!' I would rather wait till they say, not without caution: 'Look how I look at you . . .' I let Jacques get on with it. But as I really do seem to have taken refuge somewhere deep inside me, in order to return to reality I have to pass through a sort of foetal state. I curl to grab the hardened member so that my lips can feel the soft envelope which slides over its axis. I can mobilise myself into this act so utterly that I feel full up to the brim, my entire body has been put on and filled out like a glove.

In a series of images taken by an American photographer, who published some of them many years later in the magazine *On Seeing*, I can be seen – I can see myself today – first standing like a fragile sleepwalker (almost as if I am swaying) next to a couple fornicating on a mattress. It is dark, it looks as if I am dressed entirely in black, the light falls only onto the girl's knees and the soles of the boy's feet. In other shots I am sitting next to the couple, bent in two; you can just make out, under a crop of hair, that my head is squeezed between the girl's

thigh and the boy's hips. I must be trying to lick whatever parts of their conjoined genitals I can reach. What do I look like? A conscientious workman – plumber, decorator, mechanic – examining the areas where his intervention is needed; a child whose toy has rolled under the bed and who searches the darkness to find it; an exhausted runner who sits down and drops his chest forward before catching his breath. I can confirm that the effort I put into introducing my body into the space between their two bodies (and you could be forgiven for thinking I want to insert it whole) is matched by intense mental concentration.

4. DETAILS

I really like sucking a man off. I was initiated in this virtually at the same time as I learned to direct the exposed glans towards the other, subterranean, entrance. In my naivety I initially thought that a blow-job was a deviant sexual practice. I can still hear myself describing the thing to a dubious and slightly disgusted girl friend; I tried to affect indifference when I was actually rather proud of my discovery and my aptitude for coping. This aptitude is very difficult to explain because, over and above whatever vestiges there may be of the oral stage, and before the challenge put into accomplishing an act which you believe to be abnormal, there is an obscure identification with the member you appropriate. During an exploration carried out simultaneously with fingers and tongue you come to know every last detail of its topography and even its tiniest reactions – perhaps better than its very owner. As a result there is a feeling of in-effable mastery: a tiny quivering of the end of the tongue, and you unleash a disproportionate response. Added to this is the fact that taking something right into your mouth gives you a more thorough feeling of being filled than when it is the vagina that is occupied. The feeling in the vagina is diffuse, radiating outwards, the occupant

seems to melt there, whereas you can perfectly distinguish the gentle proddings of the glans with the inside or the outside of the lips, on the tongue, the palate and even in the throat. Not to mention the fact that, in the final phase, you taste the sperm. In short, you are touched as subtly as you yourself touch. But for me there still remains the mystery of the transmission of sensation from one orifice to the other. How is it that the effects of suction can be felt the other end of the body, that the way the lips squeeze around the penis causes a rigid bracelet to form round the mouth of the vagina? When I perform fellatio really well, taking my time, at leisure to adjust my position and vary my rhythm, I can feel an impatience rising from some source within my body, flowing and concentrating enormous muscular energy in that place of which I have only a vague image, on the edge of this abyss which opens me up so overwhelmingly. The aperture of a barrel ringed with steel. When the ring is forged by contamination from arousal of the nearby clitoris I can understand it. But when the order comes from the mouth! The explanation undoubtedly lies in some detour via the mind. Even though I may have my eyes closed most of the time, they are so close to this meticulous work that I *see* all the same, and the image I have of it is a powerful activator of my desire. The fantasy may also revolve around the fact that, lying just behind the eyes, the brain has perfect and instantaneous intelligence of the thing so nearly touching it! First of all I see the actions which determine my breathing: the flexible channel of my hand, my lips folded over my teeth so as not to hurt, my tongue which quickly dabs the glans as it comes closer. I evaluate their progress visually, the whole hard moving with the lips, sometimes

with a slight twisting movement, and increasing the pressure when it reaches the thicker bud at the end. Then suddenly the hand goes its own way to rub swiftly up and down, forming a pincer with just two fingers, making the silky tip bob against the cushioned surface of my lips pursed into a kiss. Jacques always lets out a brief, clear little 'ha' of surprised delight (even though he knows the manoeuvre perfectly well), which redoubles my own excitement, when the hand releases its grip, allowing the organ to disappear to the back of my throat. I try to keep it there for a moment and even to manoeuvre its rounded tip over the back of my palate until tears come to my eyes, until I'm suffocating. Or – but for this you need your whole body to be well balanced – I hold the hub still and gravitate my whole head round it, distributing gentle strokes from my cheeks, my chin moistened with saliva, my forehead, hair and even the end of my nose. I lick lavishly right down to the balls which you can take into your mouth whole. These movements are punctuated by longer halts on the glans where the tip of the tongue describes circles, unless it decides instead to devote itself to niggling at the edge of the foreskin. Then, bang! Without any warning I take the whole thing back into my mouth and I hear the cry which transmits its wave down to the cast iron ring forged around the entry to my cunt.

It would be easy for me to write pages about this, especially as just describing this painstaking job has already triggered the first signs of excitement. There might even be a distant link between my attention to detail in a blow-job and the care I take over each description in my writing. I will restrict myself to adding that I also like giving up my role as the driving force. I like to have my

head held still by two firm hands and to be fucked into my mouth the way I can be fucked in my cunt. In general, I feel the need to take a man into my mouth in the first few moments of a sexual encounter, just to titillate those few millilitres of blood which produce the erection. Either we are standing and I let myself drop down at my partner's feet, or we are lying down and I quickly make my way under the sheet. It is like a game. I go into the dark looking for the thing I want. And in fact, in these moments, I have a silly tendency to talk like a greedy child. I ask for 'my big lollipop' and it gives me a kick. And when I lift my head up, because I do have to relax the muscles sucked in along the insides of my cheeks, I stick to the 'umm . . . it's good' of someone establishing that their taste buds are enjoying something they are eating. By the same token, I receive all compliments with the same vanity as a good pupil on prize day. Nothing pleases me more than hearing that I 'give the best blow-job'. Better than that: when, with a view to writing this book, I talk to a friend 25 years after my sexual relationship with him ended and I hear him say that he has 'never met a girl who could suck a man off so well', I lower my eyes, in some ways out of modesty, but also to hide my pride. It is not that I have been deprived of other forms of gratification in my personal or professional life but, as far as I can see, there is a balance to be sustained between the acquisition of moral and intellectual qualities which earns the respect of our peers, and a proportional excellence in practices which flout these qualities, brush them aside and deny them. We can demonstrate this ability to such an extent that we wouldn't mind seeing the admiration it inspires turning to mockery. Éric nearly punched one

narrow-minded idiot we met one evening in the club called the Cleopatra. When I was offered something to drink, the idiot – who wasn't up to appreciating my enthusiasm in a fitting manner – announced that it was about time because the place was beginning to 'smell of burned rubber'.

The body in pieces

If each of us drew our own body as if by dictation from our own internal perspective, we would produce a real gallery of monsters! I myself would be hydrocephalic and callipygian, and these two protuberances would be joined by an insubstantial mollusc-like arm (I have trouble making my breasts count for anything), and the whole thing would be planted on two posts which impede movement more than they facilitate it (I have had a complex about my legs for a long time). Perhaps it's my cerebral nature which has led me to according priority to the organs of the head, the eyes and the mouth. There could even be a compensatory relationship between them. When I was very young people used to compliment me for my big eyes; people noticed them because they were dark brown. As I grew up my eyes became proportionately less important within my face and, as an adolescent, my wounded narcissism had to accept that no one made so much fuss about them any more. So I made my mouth, which I thought was rather fetching, a possible means of attraction. And I learned to open it wide, closing my eyes at the same time, at least in certain circumstances, while my backside came to represent the image I had of myself,

181

its rotundity all the more accentuated by my pronounced waist. This backside which I extend ever further into the unknown regions of the *outback* (the name Australians give to the desert that lies behind them), which I will never see. Jacques once gave me a postcard of a sketch Picasso made for *Les Demoiselles d'Avignon*: a woman seen from behind, her torso the shape of an isosceles triangle, her buttocks curving dramatically above knuckles of ham. My portrait, said he.

My arse, another side of who I am. Claude used to say I had a 'so-so face, but what an arse!' I like it when Jacques is on the job and he uses the word arse un-specifically to designate the whole lower part of my body which he is penetrating, and when he accompanies his declarations of love addressed to it with sharp slaps on my buttocks. I make a point of asking for this sort of attention. 'Do for my arse' is one of my most frequent requests. In response, he grabs my buttocks and shakes their malleable mass as if he were trying to whip up two mountains of cream. If he finishes off the job by inserting two fingers in a duck's head formation and then opens the bill – i.e. parts the two fingers – in the narrow corridor which leads from the parting of the buttocks to the open-ing of the cunt, then I'm well ready to be shafted.

Once done over, I too can get going. Whether I am lying down or on all fours, I play energetically on the suppleness of my waist, and the repercussions of my regular, vigorous thrusts provoke the fantasy melding of my mouth and my genitals. I want to know whether I am 'sucking' him well with my cunt. 'Am I going to suck up all your cum?' The answer I hope for subsumes my identity to that part of me in which all of me is

concentrated: 'Oh, Catherine! Your arse, your arse ...'
Knowing that what I cannot see myself is being attentively
examined is just as stimulating. A focused ray of light
(from an adjustable bedside light, for example) is preferable to more diffuse lighting. I have been known to
suggest using a torch. By glancing back I can see the
expression on a man's face as he scrutinises the cleft
between my buttocks which facilitates the disappearance
of his precious appendage. I rely heavily on the
description he gives me, however literal and crude it may
be. 'Can you see my arse?' 'Ah, yes, it's lovely you know,
it's really taking in my dick. Huh, the little fucker wants
more ...' If there happens to be a mirror nearby, if I put
myself in profile, I myself can oversee the immersion and
emergence of what looks like a piece of flotsam tossed by
the swell. Because of this predilection for sensations in my
rump, the doggie position has been my favourite for a
long time, until I ended up admitting to myself – we
always end up being sexually honest with ourselves, but
this can, of course, take a long time – that, even though it
allowed the rod to strike deep and hard, it still wasn't the
form of penetration that satisfied me the most. In other
words, having gone in pursuit of the dick with the
energetic buckings of my hips, and having been alternately
pinned down and buffed up like a polisher's duster, I like
to be turned over and shagged in the classic position.

The pleasure I take in exposing my arse goes back a
long time. When I was six or seven I would expose it to
my brother in a game which included some of the moves
I used to masturbate. That is, with my skirt hitched up, I
would crease my knickers up into the front of my crack,
and I would push my buttocks out as far as I could

beyond the back of the little bench I was sitting on. Then I would wait for the little chap to go behind me. What amused us about it was that I would pretend to have revealed myself quite absent-mindedly, and he pretended to brush my buttocks inadvertently.

It must be that we give caresses the way that we receive them because I have always responded eagerly to men with sensitive arses. I have mentioned the friend who offered himself on all fours for me to finger-fuck him until my arm and shoulder were paralysed with pain. Another once planted his buttocks on my nose without any warning. It was at the beginning of our relationship, he was being coy, I had to overcome his resistance before I could undertake fellatio. But I had hardly taken him into my mouth when his body stiffened and he pivoted round and presented me with two resolute buttocks. It was easier for me to get to his arsehole than his glans. Even so, when I got back up, I thought he still had the same severe, almost reproving, expression that he had assumed when I first introduced him into my mouth. After that, I got into the habit of exploring this man's body in minute detail; I have never licked, kissed and nibbled anyone so thoroughly from his earlobes to the shifting skin attaching his testicles, via the delicate depressions under his arms, in the crooks of his elbows and in the folds of his groin. It was the systematic occupation of a territory where I left my mark in the form of tiny gobs of spit released from a few centimetres to give the limpid saliva time to extend, the sign of a soiling.

Is it because people were less interested in my bosom that it is more lymphatic by nature, and is it because I never thought to offer it spontaneously to be seen and

fondled by others that I find it annoying having to stimulate my partner's nipples? A lot of men ask you to 'do
their tits' and they even expect this coaxing to take the
form of pinching and biting these delicate areas. I have
regularly been reproached for not pinching hard enough
when my hand hurt from rolling nipples between my
fingers at the same time as I tried to squeeze them. Not
only is the sadistic the least developed of my impulses, I
can't find any resonance in myself for pleasure provoked
in this way. Personally, I prefer my breasts to be enveloped
in a wider, more subtle gesture, which is even nicer at the
time in my cycle when my breasts are heavier because then
I can feel them quivering gently. I don't like them to be
pressed or pinched. Any rubbing of my nipples I keep for
myself, and then only to feel how hard and knobbly they
are under my smooth palms. But in my own intimacy, I
can experience an even more striking contrast: kneeling or
on all fours, I rub my breasts on my thighs, and this is a
confusing feeling; it feels as if my own thighs are strangers
to me, as if they don't belong to me, that their touch
comes from outside me, and I melt, always surprised by
their velvety skin.

On the subject of seeking out a contrast between rough
surfaces and soft ones, I have just remembered one of the
very first times I experienced an erotic emotion as such.
My brother and I would be sent to spend a holiday with
some friends of my father's whose numerous grand-
children played with us. One day, the grandfather, who
was ill, had to go to bed and I went to see him in his room.
As I sat on the edge of the bed, he started to examine my
face. Feeling his way with his fingers, he commented that
I had a very fine jawbone; when he reached my neck he

diagnosed that later in life I might be susceptible to goitre. These contradictory observations worried me. Then, slipping his hand under my blouse, he brushed past my breasts which were barely beginning to bud. And as I stayed there silent and motionless he said that, when I became a woman, I would really like it when people stroked my 'titties' in this way. I still didn't move, or perhaps just my head which I turned towards the wall as if I couldn't hear what I was being told. The callused surface of his big hand snagged on my skin. I was aware for the first time of the stiffening of my nipple. I listened to the prediction. I was suddenly brought to the threshold of womanhood and I felt a sense of pride. A child forges its power in the enigma of its future life. So, though disconcerted by this gesture for which I had no ready-made response, I turned back to look at this man, who I was fond of, on his bed. I felt sorry for him because his wife was crippled, obese, her legs were covered in suppurating sores which he dressed meticulously morning and evening. At the same time his greyish face and his lumpy nose made me want to laugh. I extricated myself gently.

That evening, lying in the bed that I shared with one of his granddaughters, I told her about the episode. He had touched her too. We looked each other right in the eye as we spoke, trying to measure the magnitude of our discovery in the other's gaze. We were pretty sure the grandfather was doing something forbidden, but the secret that he gave us to share was far more valuable than some moral whose meaning was, anyway, no clearer. When I once decided – again with a sense of pride, almost bravado – to talk about my masturbating in confession, the priest's reaction was so disappointing (he made

absolutely no comment and just gave me a few *aves* and the odd *Pater* to recite as usual) that I felt nothing but contempt for him afterwards. So, trying to tell him that I had been stirred because an old man had put his hand on my breast . . . !

If I see a man's eyes alighting – even just for half a second – on the place where I deduce that my bra is straining the buttons of my blouse, or more usually, if I am talking to someone whose eyes fixed on me are apparently following a train of thought unrelated to the one I am informing him about, I always take refuge in exactly the same modest behaviour as in that first examination by the grandfather. For the same reason you won't find any low cut or tight-fitting dresses in my wardrobe. This modesty extends even to those around me. If I were sitting on a sofa in someone's sitting room next to a woman in very revealing clothes, I would instinctively pull down the hem of my own skirt and hunch over my breasts. In this sort of situation, my discomfiture derives as much from the impression that, by association, it is my own anatomy that she is revealing, as from my tendency – described earlier – to break down the barriers of sexual contact from the word go; by adjusting my clothes, I am stopping myself from burying my hands between the two half exposed breasts and revealing them in their entirety. And yet I myself wore no underwear at all for many years. I can't remember why I gave up using it. It was definitely not to follow the feminists who wanted us all to burn our bras, because I never adhered to that philosophy, but it was perhaps in the same spirit of rejecting accessories of seduction. Obviously, the results could have the opposite of the desired effect, breasts which can be seen moving

freely under clothes are just as tantalising – although, more 'naturally' – as those shown off to best effect by a bra. I could at least feel free from any suspicion of having a battle plan for my conquests. I passed up on knickers in the same way. For how many years was I compelled, for reasons of hygiene, to clean the crotch of my trousers every evening, when it would have been much quicker to put a pair of knickers in the washing machine? I just thought it was much simpler to slip all my other clothes on. This tendency was dictated to me by a minimalist, almost functionalist principle: the principle according to which a free body need not weigh itself down with ornamentation, as long as it is ready without the need for any preliminaries, no shedding of lace or manipulating of hooks. To recap, I don't like it when a man undresses me with his gaze but, once you get down to undressing for real, then it might as well be in one swift move.

If a subjective eye were on a journey, what a world of contrasts it would see! Like a mountain road interrupted by tunnels, you pass abruptly from darkness into light, and from the light into darkness. Here I am trying to explain that I prefer to keep covered something which it is perfectly acceptable to reveal, when within these same pages I have displayed an intimacy that most people keep secret. It is obvious that, in the same way that psycho-analysis helps you to shed unwanted parts of yourself, when you write a book in the first person the latter becomes the third person. The more I describe my body and my actions, the more I leave myself behind. Who recognises themselves in those magnifying mirrors which show cheeks and noses as vast fissured landscapes? Because sexual pleasure brings you outside your own

limits, it can impose the same sort of distance. Perhaps there is even a structural relationship, and the distance governs the pleasure as much as it is governed by it, at least for the category of creature to which I belong. Because, and this is the point I wanted to make, the same woman whom I described as uncomfortable under someone's insistent gaze, and who hesitated to wear suggestive clothes, the same woman in fact who partook blind in sexual adventures with faceless partners, this same woman, then, takes indisputable pleasure in exposing herself on condition that the exposure is distanced at once, by a narrative.

Image and language are in cahoots. It is so stimulating to look in a mirror and measure – to the nearest centimetre – the amount of flesh that your own flesh can swallow, and this is because the show gives rise to words. 'Oh my! It's going in so smoothly, so deep! – Hang on, I'm going to leave it there so that you can really see it, I'll do the business later . . .' One kind of dialogue that Jacques and I adopted willingly can be characterised by its purely factual being. If the vocabulary is crude and limited, this is less to do with a desire to provoke each other by upping the obscenity stakes than a need to be accurate in our descriptions. 'Can you feel how wet I am? Even my thighs are soaked, and my little clit's all swollen.' 'God, you move your arse well! Does it want my prick? Does it?' 'Yes, but I want to feel your knob on my clit again first, can I rub you against it?' 'Yes, and afterwards we're going to give the arse a good ramming!' 'That's good. How about you, does your dick like it?' 'Yes, he likes it.' 'Is it pulling on your balls too?' 'Yes, it's pumping them really well. But, hey, we're going to give this cunt another

really good thrust, aren't we?' And so the exchange goes on in a tone of voice which remains, even as we approach the conclusion, fairly measured. In so far as we don't see or feel the same thing at the same time, each speaks to the other with the intention of adding to their knowledge. You could also say that we were like two dubbing actors, their eyes riveted on the screen where they watch the actions of the characters to whom they give their voices: with our words we relay the actions of the protagonists in the porn film we are watching, and whose names are Arse, Cunt, Balls and Prick.

Narration cuts bodies into pieces, satisfies the need to reify them, to instrumentalise them. That famous scene in Godard's *Le Mépris,* when Piccoli runs, word by word, over Bardot's body, is a beautiful transposition of the two-way traffic between sight and speech, each word bringing a part of the body into focus. How many times don't people say 'Look!' when they're fucking? Of course you are at your leisure to see things close at hand, but in order to see well we sometimes also need to stand back, the way we move back from an exhibit in a museum. Undressing, I love to gaze on a promising-looking cock. Abiding by the law of the Gestalt Theory, it looks enormous in relation to the body which becomes almost fragile in its – sometimes laughable – semi-nudity and its unexpected isolation in the middle of the room; in any event the cock certainly looks bigger than it would if I were looking at it on its own. In the same way, I can, without any warning, break out of the game and go and stand a couple of metres away, with my back turned, my hands forced onto my buttocks to spread them as far apart as possible, bringing into the same sight line both the brownish crater of the

arsehole and the crimson valley of the vulva. Like when an invitation takes on the wording of a necessity, as in: 'you must taste these fruits', so 'you must look at my arse'. And because things are more picturesque if they are animated, I make it quiver.

To show my arse and to see my face. There are few pleasures to equal this double polarisation. The layout of the bathroom is perfect: while the basin offers a perfect gripping point to deaden the shocks to my rear-end, I intermittently catch sight of my harshly lit face in the mirror above it, a face which – quite unlike the lower half of my body, which is totally mobilised – is almost lifeless. The cheeks are hollow and the mouth half open like an automated doll when the mechanism winds down. It could be the face of a dead woman except for my gaze which is intolerably listless. I try both to avoid it by lowering my eyelids and seek it out. That gaze is the anchoring point; it is by seeing its reflection that I establish this certainty: there I am, that is me coming. It is the siphon through which all of me is evacuated: I cannot recognise myself in such a state of release; I reject it with a feeling of shame. That is how pleasure stays on a knife-edge: just as the multiplication of two negative numbers gives a positive number, this pleasure is the product not, as is sometimes said, of an absence from oneself, but of the bringing together of this perceived absence and the feeling of horror that it provokes in a flash of conscience. Sometimes I bring myself to this peak of pleasure all by myself, as an interval in washing myself. With one hand on the edge of the basin and the other one masturbating, I watch myself in the mirror out of the corner of my eye. A particular porn film made quite an impression on me.

The man was taking the woman from behind. The camera was facing her so that her face was in the foreground. Thanks to the pressure exerted on her whole body, her face was projected forwards and distorted as things are when they come too close to the lens. You could hear the man's orders: 'Look! Look at the camera!', and the girl looked directly at you, the viewer. I thought he might well be pulling her hair to force her to raise her head. This scene has given me a lot of inspiration for the little scenarios which nourish my masturbating. In real life, a man that I met only once gave me such intense pleasure that I have very precise memories of it, and this was because with every thrust he would order me 'Look me in the eye'. I did as I was told, knowing that he was witness to the decomposition of my face.

An ability to absorb

One weakness of porn films is to present stereotyped images of orgasm; the characters always come after a series of accelerated jerks, eyes closed, mouths open, and screaming. Now, orgasms can happen with no movement at all and in silence, and you can watch them building up and then unfold. It is usually when you want to fire up or stimulate desire that – in life as in films – you resort to clichés. Pretty much the same words, obscene or not, come to everyone. Men frequently order partners to ask for them and their organs ('Do you want a big one? Answer me', 'Call me, go on, call me'), whereas women, even the most independent-minded, tend towards subjection, even to the extent of asking for what would be

horrible injuries ('Stab it into me!', 'Go on, tear me open!'). Seeing myself in a video spreading the cum which has just spurted onto me all over my breasts, I wonder whether I am not just repeating something I have seen dozens of times on the screen. The jet was not as frothy as in the films but it was nevertheless spectacular; the spunk makes my skin shine. Did men and women use the same rhetoric and was their erotic repertoire the same before the invention of cinema? But the more powerful the orgasm, the less 'hamming it up' there is. I can confirm that in my own case. While the level of pleasure is rising, I take a very active part. As well as moving my hips, I use my arms and legs. If I am lying on my back, I spur on my partner by repeatedly kicking my heels on his buttocks and thighs. Then I reach a stage when this frantic level of activity drops. My partner is now concentrating on only one inert parcel of flesh. My voice sounds quite different. We have already abandoned our running commentary, the words we exchange become more laconic. I say 'yes, yes, yes, yes,' sometimes accompanying this litany with rapid movements of my head from left to right, or I keep saying 'go on, go on'. And, suddenly, my voice becomes higher, louder, with the clarity and authority of an actor who has learned to project their voice, and the words are more spaced out, the syllables more emphatic, 'keep go-ing'. Sometimes the 'yes' becomes a 'no' and in some images I see myself burying my face in my hands.

I wouldn't do the job that I do, nor would I be capable of gathering together all these notes if I did not have some gift for observation. A gift put to greater effect because it is coupled with a solid superego. I don't let myself go easily and, in those moments when you are supposed to be

completely passive, I am often still alert. I have, therefore, always paid very close attention to my partners, to those who had an identity of course, but also whatever level our relationship, a deep and lasting attachment or a passing affair. This degree of attention surely belongs to the same perceptive structure as the concentration I display in front of a painting, or my ability – in the metro, a restaurant or a waiting room – to lose myself completely in my contemplation of the people sitting next to me. An attention that defines my know-how. I take pride in the fact that I am quite an expert and I have become one because I have always been aware of the effects my initiatives produce. As I have described at the beginning of this chapter, I have spontaneously slipped under other people's skins in an effort to myself feel what they were feeling. That is not just a turn of phrase; I have surprised myself mimicking habits and exclamations that were peculiar to someone else. Which amounts to saying that I often relegated my own pleasure to the background. It took me a long time, a really long time, to identify the caresses, the positions that I liked best. I will venture this as an explanation: I was not right from the start granted a body predisposed to pleasure. First I had to give myself – literally abandon my whole body – to sexual activity, to lose myself in it so thoroughly that I confused myself with my partner so that I could emerge from this transformation having sloughed off the body I was given at birth and taken on a second body, one capable of taking as much as it could give. In the meantime, I lost myself in the contemplation of many faces and bodies.

With very few exceptions, I can remember with relative accuracy the bodies of my main partners, and even what

their faces retained at the moment when the other part of their being was released. These images are accompanied by memories of the convulsive movements and particular choice of words each of them had. Observation does not automatically lead to judgement but, if it is scrupulous, it keeps conscience in the realms of objectivity. I may have been seduced by a man's physical beauty, but that wouldn't stop me from identifying flaws which could cut short any fascination for him. For example, a roundish face set off with almond eyes but mounted on a head that was very flattened at the back which when I looked at it in profile brought to mind a squashed balloon. A quarter turn and the man whose face could be compared to a Renaissance painting really had no more depth than a picture on canvas. If I run back through a portrait gallery, I can find fault with my memory and my powers of observation: paradoxically, there was one man whose good looks were particularly seductive to me (in fact the only man of all my sexual contacts who was younger than me) but I have no sexual memories of him. I can call to mind lots of expressions and gestures he made and plenty of things that he said, but not one of them would have occured while we were fucking!

Was nature trying to spare men the danger of being torn in two when she ordained that, while their muscles are strained to their limits, this tension is compensated by bathing their faces in peace? Doesn't it look as if they are throwing their faces back to refresh them under a fountain in that instant when they come to the end of the pursuit that has exercised their entire body? Many of them adopt this serene expression: not the man who looked like a Renaissance portrait. While there is a whole succession of

peaceful faces in my memory – one making a little 'o' with his mouth and, because he had a moustache, looking as daft as a child in disguise; another whose smile was so half-hearted that it could have been a sign of embarrass-ment, the sort of smile a modest person would wear as they apologised for being caught in some indecent act – or again, this other man whose face was usually so smooth who wore a mask of suppressed pain. He would have seemed pitiable if in those moments he hadn't added to the usual exclamation of 'I'm coming, I'm coming!' the words 'oh, my God!' A comical invocation that I could not not notice.

But calm can also be mistaken for indifference. I knew one man who was so contemplative that he withdrew completely from his physical appearance to the extent that it no longer expressed anything. His body rested on me with all its weight; yes, it was active but impassive, as if he had abandoned it to me, and this absent face would park next to mine while I watched his ghost transported by orgasm floating above us like in a fantasy film. It was the same body that I saw when this man masturbated, indifferent to my presence and using a technique unique to him. He would lie on his tummy with his arms bent by his sides and squeeze his organ between his strong muscular thighs by contracting them. It was a stocky body, and the muscles stood out all the more in this position. Myself an experienced expert of onanism, I admired the concen-tration he applied to the job, stubbornly and defiantly defending the mental isolation it requires.

When you have made love with a man a few times, you recognise when he is going to 'come', even if he is not one of those who announce it out loud. Perhaps you know

before he does, informed by tiny signs: perhaps because he has slipped you into a position which acts like a trigger on him; perhaps because he falls silent, his breathing becomes audible, appeased a few moments in advance. One friend who was an imaginative, talkative and active fucker, who would keep you there for an hour with his extraordinary erotic fabulations and would make you try out the most acrobatic positions and the most improbable substitutes (cucumbers, sausages, Perrier bottles, policeman's luminous white truncheon, etc.), would suddenly become quiet a few moments before orgasm. Whatever position I was in, he would bring me back underneath him, start to file without forcing and replace words with discreet little moans. I was convinced that this final phase followed a decision taken with full knowledge of the facts and I wouldn't have been surprised to have heard him say: 'Right, that's enough fun and games, let's get down to business.' Afterwards, when he had discharged, he would stay on top of me, unleashing a little 'hi, hi, hi' in my ear which sounded like a forced laugh, but was more probably his way of gently returning us to the real world. It was the laugh of someone who laughs first, in the hopes of finding your complicity and your forgiveness for having dragged you on some unexpected escapade. And, as if to help extract me from our dream, before he opened his eyes, he would scratch my scalp affectionately.

In the same way that I don't take exception to flirting with abjection, that this nourishes my fantasies, that I have never been put off titillating the folds of an anus with my tongue ('Hmm! It smells of shit,' I hear myself saying, 'but it's good'), and that I have willingly cast myself as a 'bitch on heat', neither am I disgusted – far from it – if I

can feast my eyes on a body that may be in some way damaged. Yes, I like it when the whole body in my arms is as firm as a well polished dick, but, yes, I am also just as happy to slither under the drooping gut of a man I have just suckled as he waits in a female position. Yes, I value the abilities of a man who spreads the lips of the vulva with careful surgeon's fingers and who takes the time to admire what he finds with a connoisseur's relish, before he brings you off with an extraordinary precision soon unbearable. But the man who grabs your hips with about as much ceremony as if he were snatching hold of the rail on a listing boat is just as welcome! And the one who mounts you with the vacant distant expression of a mating animal! The one who virtually lies full length on your back, gripping the fat of your buttocks so hard that you find bruises on them the next day, and who doesn't give a toss that you can only keep your balance thanks to excruciating cramp in your thighs that support the weight of two bodies. After that you let yourself go, reduced to little more than a lump of flesh, plonked onto the bed and turned over with no more response of its own than a ball of bread dough. Being the amorphous support of someone else's frenetic activity, forgetting that your own flesh can have a specific form, and watching your breasts spreading and flowing with the movement, rocked like the water in the bottom of a boat, or seeing the cellulite on your buttocks squeezed in a big pair of hands. At times like these, as my eyes float over the surface of my molten body, I have to catch the eye of this workman dazed by his obstinate labouring. That face does not do beatific ecstasy. It would frighten me if the denatured bird that I am did not fall in love with the scarecrow. One eye is half closed

because of a tensing effect which only affects half the face – I have already seen this happen to people who have had strokes – and the corresponding corner of the mouth twists to expose the gums. If I am not afraid of this snarling grimace, that is because it doesn't express pain but rather a supreme effort, a prodigious tenacity, and I am proud to submit myself to this force.

Patient

For much of my life I fucked naively. What I mean by that was that sleeping with men was a natural activity which didn't unduly bother me. Obviously, from time to time I would come across some of the attendant psychological problems (lies, wounded pride, jealousy), but they could be written off on the profit and loss account. I wasn't very sentimental. I needed affection, and I found it, but without feeling any need to go and build love stories out of sexual relationships. When I did fall for someone, I think I was still conscious of succumbing to some charm, a physical seduction, even to the geometry of relations (for example, simultaneously having affairs with a much older man and a younger man, and having fun shifting from playing the role of a little girl to that of a protector) without ever being fully engaged. When I complained how difficult it was managing four or five sustained relationships at once, I had a good friend who would tell me that it wasn't the number of men that was difficult but finding a balance between them, and he would recommend that I took a sixth. So I just left everything up to chance. I paid no more attention to the quality of sexual relationships. In

cases where they didn't give me much pleasure, or they even bothered me in some way, or when the man made me do things which weren't really to my liking, that wasn't reason enough to call them into question. In most cases, it was the friendship in the relationship that was most important. It could obviously lead to a sexual relationship, and I even found that reassuring; I needed to sense that all of me was appreciated. Whether or not I found immediate sensory satisfaction was less important. That too was written off on the balance sheet. I wouldn't be exaggerating if I said that, until I was about 35, I had not imagined that my own pleasure could be the aim of a sexual encounter. That I hadn't understood.

My hardly romantic attitude never stopped me from handing out 'I love you's to my heart's content, only at the precise moment when the little motor situated in my partner's groin revved up. Or I would keep saying his name out loud. I don't know what made me think that that would encourage him to pursue and achieve his pleasure. I was all the more prodigal with these purely opportune declarations of love because they remained on the surface, uttered neither under the effects of any emotion, nor because I was carried away in my ecstasy. I clear-headedly applied what I believed to be a technical device. As time goes by, we do away with this sort of artifice.

Romain was very gentle, almost indolent underneath a virile outward appearance, his leather jacket slung over a bachelor's un-ironed T-shirt. Yet another who lived in a studio on Saint-Germain-des-Prés, the least cluttered one I knew. We fucked on a mattress on the carpet, in the middle of the room, as the overhead light hit me full on.

The first time I kept on looking at the light bulb and didn't realise that he'd ejaculated. Weightless, his chest lay over mine, his head turned away. The only living thing that I could feel was the odd strand of his long hair brushing over my mouth and chin. I had hardly felt him penetrate, he had scarcely executed a few weak thrusts. I too lay motionless, embarrassed. I wouldn't have wanted to disturb him if he hadn't finished, but if that was the case wasn't it my job to make my presence known and get him going again? But if I started moving after he had done would I not look stupid? Eventually I felt something running right at the top of my thigh, a bit of sperm spat out by my vagina. Romain's organ was a good size, it got off quite happily but it was completely passive. If I had wanted to personify his cock, I could have compared it to a novice who doesn't move from his chair when all the participants in a ceremony rise to their feet: you felt no more the urge to rebuke him than you would the inept novice. As I spread my legs under this youth, I had almost a sense of comfort from feeling nothing, nothing nice, but nothing nasty either.

In some situations I can display a rare patience. I have in me sufficient resources to remain silent and give my mind a free reign, accepting the fact that others are living their lives alongside me. I can cope uncomplainingly with the manias, petty tyrannies or even outright attacks of others and I can turn inwards when necessary. I let them get on and do my thing. Looking back on it, I now realise just how patient I proved to be in sexual relationships. Feeling nothing, not minding and accomplishing well the whole ritual to its conclusion. Not getting hung up about the same tastes as my partner, and getting on with it, etc.

Indifferent because mentally so well tucked away at my very core that I could control my body as a puppeteer does a puppet. So I went on seeing Romain. Thanks to the impression he gave of being a bastard with tenderness he had quite a lot of success with women, and I enjoyed imagining the surprise or the disappointment of those who thought they were about to do it with a stud. I saw the astonished eyes of one of these women, probing mine for the comfort afforded by sharing a disappointing experience: 'But Romain . . . he doesn't move!' I listened to the destroyed creature with the calm of a sage.

I have spoken of the boredom that sometimes gripped me when meeting up with friends, and of the escape route I discovered by going off with one of them for a fuck. But fucking can be boring! Still, I prefer that particular boredom. I take in my stride a cunnilingus that neither turns me on or off, decide against redirecting a finger which fails to find my clitoris, and finally, I can be perfectly happy when my partner comes even if I myself don't get much out of it because, in the long run, this being not quite on the button is a drag; I can tolerate all that so long as either before or afterwards the conversation is stimulating, my dinner partners are unusual, or I can wander round an apartment I really like, pretending I am living a different life . . . My train of thought is so absent from contingencies that it won't be hampered by a mere body, even if that body is wrapped in the arms of another body. Better still, the thought is all the freer if whoever you are talking to is concentrating on the body; surely it isn't then going to resent him for using it as an erotic accessory!

It is not necessarily womanisers who best satisfy women. It may even be that some of them – although not

all – go from one woman to the next in order only ever to experience beginnings and to spare themselves the stage when some sort of fulfilment is required. (No doubt you could say the same of some man-eating women . . .) One of the first that I met, an artist, was also much older than me, and one of my friends had warned me: 'When men are a bit older, it's fantastic, they're so experienced that you don't have to do anything, just open up your legs!' I had to make quite an effort not to contradict her. In one of the rooms in his artist's studio, the one in which he received visitors, there was a big table laden with things. It was like a house of curiosities with a jumble of ornaments, lamps, vases, exotic shaped bottles and kitsch ashtrays as well as unusual tools and plans and sketches for his own work. We often didn't bother to go as far as the bedroom, I would go and mingle with this bric-a-brac. He would push me up against the table. Was it because he was slightly shorter than me that I can remember his half-closed eyelids so clearly, the bags under his eyes like a reflection of his eyelids, and his childish, begging expression? Our pelvises were more or less level and, as soon as I felt the swelling under his trousers I would get my 'little motor', as he called it, going. That is, I, as I was wont, would jerk my hips rhythmically. And he would respond to these movements, so that we rubbed our pubic regions against each other. What ramblings did my mind go off on once my excitement started to fade? Would I notice a new picture pinned to the wall? Would I think about the article I had to write, or instead did I empty my mind and stare at the little excrescences of brown skin on the surface of his eyelids? Did I think about the fact that we would have time to do this again later and that then

his organ would go so far as to penetrate mine? He threw his head back, he pushed me a little harder against the table which dug into my buttocks, and let out a couple of little whinnies. We could leave it at that.

And yet he was an attentive man and, while I took him and his friends as they came, he would examine me – as he examined everyone – with a piercing gaze. I have never known a man to be less easy going in the comments he made about your body, and these comments would be uttered without ulterior motive, but with the exactitude of a professional eye, and whatever flaws you might have would anyway not detract from the fact that you were a 'turn on' to him. On top of this, his visual acuity was coupled with great dexterity from which I benefited when he touched me. But others – if I can put it like this – don't bother with the body you offer them if you have already rendered them a satisfactory service. Like, for example, the man who took me to an attic room on the avenue Paul-Doumer which he used as his office. There he was pawing me – that wasn't what I came for, but OK. The normal procedure would see him taking me to the couch and lying me down on it. Well, no, he is the one who lies down on it, full length on his back, swooning and, with what is always a rather pathetic gesture, holds out his prick without looking at it. So I take the latter in my mouth and quite soon I hear him say: 'Oh, I'm going to come! With you, I don't stand on ceremony with you, I'll take you later.' As far as I am concerned, I can handle this but my mind is sufficiently alert to realise that he is behaving badly. He doesn't take me later.

I am docile not because I like submission, I have never tried to put myself in a masochistic situation, but out of

indifference to the uses to which we put our bodies. Of course, I would never have given myself over to extreme practices such as inflicting or suffering pain, but apart from that, given the enormous scope of individual preferences – sexual eccentricities even – I always had an open mind and I was invariably well up for it in mind and body. At the most I could have been blamed for a lack of conviction if someone's practices didn't find much resonance in my own fantasies. For a long time I used to see a man who now and then felt the need to pee over me. I knew what to expect when he made me get out of bed to suck him off. When his organ was good and hard, he would take it out and hold it with one hand, not far from me. I kept my mouth open. Kneeling there in front of him like that I must have looked like someone about to take communion. There was always a brief pause during which he seemed to be mentally guiding the urine on its way. With this effort of concentration he managed not to come. And the jet streamed onto me, full, firm and hot. Bitter. So bitter I have never tasted its equal, strong enough to make you retract your tongue all the way to the back of your throat. He manipulated his organ the way he would have done a hose pipe and the flow was so abundant and lasted such a long time that I sometimes really had to duck and dive the way you would if someone were trying to spray you with water. Once when I lay down under the stream, when he had finished he came to lay down on the floor with me. Using both hands, he daubed me all over with his piss and covered me with kisses. I hate the feeling of wet hair on my neck but there was nothing I could do to stop it trickling. I burst out laughing. This made him angry, and brought his affections to an abrupt end. Years

later he still held it against me! 'There's one thing you're not good at, and that's being pissed on.' I admit it. In my defence, I would like to make clear that I didn't laugh as a way, for example, of shrugging off my embarrassment (it wasn't the first time I had been drenched in that way!), even less to make fun of him or of us (every reasonably original sexual exploit, far from debasing me, was in fact a source of pride, like another notch in my quest for the sexual Grail). I laughed because, unable to draw any masochistic satisfaction from the situation which I didn't find humiliating, at least I did feel a sense of jubilation rolling in a disgusting liquid substance.

Some positions are less rewarding than others for someone who likes to play the big baby, hanging on to a good sized breast. The least you can say is that I am not a dominatrix, neither morally – I have never conned a man – nor sexually – in perverse little playlets, it was never me who held the whip. And I was very uncomfortable when asked to spank people! The man I used to meet in the area around the Gare de l'Est wasn't satisfied just to lick my crack, he would lift his head from time to time and, pursing his lips, would ask to be slapped. I don't remember the words he used, on the other hand I do know that he would for the occasion call me 'my queen', which I found ridiculous. I would watch him stretching out his neck and something about his face repelled me as his features softened while he waited, including his wet lips which made him look like a drinker who gets a moustache as he downs his glass. That still didn't get me to hit him hard enough. I put a lot into it but was never able to hit him hard enough. I would go at it with a backwards and forward motion, but the thought that I might

scratch him with one of my rings held my hand back. On other occasions I would try with one hand and then the other, in the hopes of putting increasing force in each movement, but then it was difficult to stay balanced, with my buttocks as close as they could get to the edge of the bed or the chair, which meant that it wasn't easy for me to hit his head as it emerged from between my thighs. In fact I wasn't into it. Paradoxically, I am convinced that if he had pretended not to attach so much importance to it, if he had put a touch of humour into his request, or camped it up so that it became an act, I myself would have entered into the game more easily, got into it and hit him harder.

Faced with my lack of aptitude, he let it alone and I don't know whether, with other women, his masochism drove him to more demanding exploits. For me, these slapping sequences were just another delay in relationships dictated by infrequent and unscheduled rendezvous. They would prolong, even if not for very long, my wait for cock. As I have described, I would come to a rendezvous already in a state of exacerbated desire. From the very first full-on kisses, from the first moment when his arms crept up under my clothes, the pleasure was violent. Next, the unquenchable sucking rekindled my desire to an almost unbearable level. But when the moment of penetration finally came, my little internal thread had broken; I had waited too long. I should probably have looked at the cycle of my desire differently, considered his licking as a prelude, chosen to forego copulation, accepted the intervals between two rendezvous as a delicious echo of his guesses, and faced the facts: the high point was that moment when, having opened the door to me, without saying hello and while we were still muffled up in our

coats, he would crush me roughly against him. In that case, the perfectionist that I am would not have seen the slaps as something that like a schoolgirl you learn but rather I would have just got on with them like the other preliminaries, smooches and simperings, that you just do.

In matters of dominance, I prefer straddling a man lying on his back. The position has little bearing on the way partners behave in role-play. When I was very young and wanted to be clever I used to call it the 'Eiffel Tower position'. A tower straddling the river Seine, the Seine a torrent churning the tower like a tide. The piston movement up and down, the woman's buttocks making a sharp little noise every time they smack down on the man's thighs; the first convolutions of a belly dance, the calmest of movements adopted when you want to catch your breath or to prolong the fantasy; the tilting backwards and forwards, the fastest and – for me – most pleasurable movement . . . all this is almost as familiar to me as fellation. In both cases the woman controls the duration and the rhythm, which obviously gives her a double advantage: the dick reacts directly inside the cunt, and the woman's body is revealed at a favourable angle, seen from below by the man. And it is gratifying every now and again to hear someone saying: 'It's you who's fucking me . . . you fuck so well!' You come and go on the rod like a well-oiled machine. Because of this ease and control if I close my eyes I can picture the rod in me as disproportionately big and strong because it so utterly fills a cavity which itself seems to have expanded to the size of my torso, and which having been well emptied of air is a perfect fit. It is also one of the positions in which a woman can best squeeze the thing by contracting the muscles in

her vagina. These are like signals sent from afar, a way of letting the other know – while you are unashamedly making prodigious use of that which belongs to him – that still you are thinking of him.

All of these manoeuvres are impossible if a woman sitting astride a man with her cunt fully occupied then opens up her arse to let a second man penetrate her. Two friends who used to skewer me like this claimed that they could feel each other's dicks through my insides and that it was very exciting. I only ever half believed them. These relatively acrobatic positions, or positions like that one, which limit your movements in your attempts to maintain them, or even immobilise you altogether, these positions are more for show. You can amuse yourselves forming a group as models would have done at some Academy in the past, and the pleasure is fuelled more by the sight of these bodies which fit as neatly as pieces of Meccano, rather than the actual contact between them. Taken in a sandwich like that, I couldn't see a great deal.

When going at it on top, I am now careful not to lean my head too far forward. Even though my face is not too lined, I don't think it is as firm as it used to be and, if my partner's eyes were open, I wouldn't want to give him a view of my flabby cheeks. My other reservation about this position is that I can't maintain each movement for very long. In the up and down movement, the thighs are activated like levers and they tire quickly, especially if they are astride a wide pair of hips. I can keep the tilting move-ment going for longer, but the problem there is that both the very localised sensation on the front of the stomach and the precise linkage to the male movement produce (by a sort of reverberation) an imperious need for

gratification. So much so that I stop the movement, catch onto the body lying beneath me and say: 'Give it into me gently.' Three or four little thrusts, striking sharply the depths of my cunt, are all I need to feel much happiness.

I admire men who can file in and out for a good while without it doing them in. I always wonder how they manage to stay leaning on their arms like that, and to show such stamina moving their hips. And their knees, how do they manage with their knees? When I am in the dominant position that I have just described and the act is taking place on the floor, my knees start to hurt. It is the same during a long fellation if I am kneeling in front of an upright man. In fact it is when I stay the distance and give a really long blow job that it's really hell. Sometimes I let go with one or both hands, for exactly the same reason as someone doing a balancing act would, to show how well the mouth can do the job on its own, or to swiftly accelerate the movement. Then, my neck tenses and becomes painful. A stiffness, as when you go to a slow dentist, spreads to my jaw, the stretched muscles in my cheeks and lips, the more so if the size of the organ to which I am attending requires me to keep my mouth wide open. When I curl my lips inwards, my teeth leave a swollen ridge along the mucus membrane on the inside of my lips. I like that particular injury. It is hot and tasty. When my mouth is free again, I run my tongue over it with the attention of an animal licking a wound. After exerting myself, I find myself again in this exquisite pain which I deliberately heighten by pressing my tongue more firmly.

I endure all the risks of coitus in the same way, the eccentricities of each partner and the minor physical

discomforts. This can be put down to an ability to pro-
gramme the body independently of physical reactions. A
body and the mind attached to it do not live in the same
temporal sphere, and their reactions to the same external
stimuli are not always synchronised. That is how we hear
a shattering piece of news without batting an eyelid or,
conversely, we can carry on crying even after we have
taken on board the fact that everything possible has been
done to console us. If I set an assembly-line of pleasure in
motion inside me, even if my body encounters some discomforts, they will not be enough to stop the
assembly-line. In other words, I will only become aware
of the discomfort after the fact, after I seem to have
reached the pleasure, and in the aftermath you really don't
care about the discomfort, you forget it before you have
noticed it. How else could you explain the fact that for
years the same men caused me the same hassles and I
never complained or tried to avoid them? I am someone
who hates to feel wet anywhere other than under a
shower, but I have frequently been splattered with great
drops of sweat by one particular man. I have never seen
anyone sweat as much as he did. I could distinguish the
impact of each drop as it fell onto me. He didn't seem to
be bothered about feeling too hot, but I had an icy feeling
all over my soaked chest. Perhaps I compensated for this
discomfort by listening to the wet smacking of his thighs
against mine; I have always been stimulated by noises. I
could have from time to time asked him nicely to wipe
himself, but I didn't. Nor did I ever get over the allergy I
had to one particular cheek being rubbed against mine.
Given that the problem was chronic, shouldn't I have
smeared myself with cream in preparation for my

rendezvous with the owner of the cheek, who made a point of shaving carefully. No, I always came away from his flat with half my face on fire. The marks took hours to fade. It could also be that, on the subject of the discontinuity between the mind and body, in this case, my feelings of guilt for visiting this man in secret could have added to the allergic condition to make me go red. There, the mind was catching up with the body in spite of itself.

Different manifestations of pleasure

It is all the easier to write about discomforts and displeasure because they seem to distend time, and time allows us to focus. Even if they do not register with us straight away, they carve out a furrow within us which represents time. The slapping sessions never went on for long, the bathing in sweat was by no means a key element of my relationship with that man, which doesn't alter the fact that while they were going on I, active and passive, would be waiting (and watching). Talking about pleasure, extreme pleasure, is much more a work of art. Isn't it anyway commonly compared to being transported out of oneself and the world, and, therefore, outside time as well? And is there the added, aporetic problem of wanting to identify and recognise something that no one has yet described for you, or only sketchily?

In the pages above I have mentioned the truly ravishing feeling of the first physical contact, and I have also evoked how I discovered a prolonged orgasm, thanks to a dildo; finally I have tried as best I can to describe changes that occur at the aperture of my vagina which becomes as hard

as a ring of metal when my excitement is at its peak. I came across these facts relatively late on. For a large part of my life I fucked without regard to pleasure. First I should concede that, for someone who has known so many partners, no outcome was ever as guaranteed as when I sought it alone. I control the pitch of my pleasure to the nearest fraction of a second, which isn't possible when you have to take into account someone else and when you depend on their moves not your own. Here's my story. Let us say that I am a porn actress auditioning fifteen possible partners who offer themselves naked all in a row. While in my fantasy I am the officer reviewing the troops, examining each in turn and squeezing his apparatus, I rub my clitoris with the end of my middle finger and it soon becomes sticky. I feel the way it dilates. Sometimes I think it just rises up, a pointed little growth like a seedling. In fact the whole mons of Venus and vulva swell under my palm, and I can abandon my circular movements for a few seconds to prod and feel the whole as I would a pear. On with the story. I choose one and I lead him by the cock to a sort of massage table where I lie down, my pussy on the edge. At that point (but this preamble will already have taken a long time, six or eight minutes, sometimes more), my level of excitement can be extremely high. It is very localised, like a weight pulling towards the depths of my vagina and seeming to close it like the aperture of a lens. And yet I know (but where does this knowledge come from? From spontaneously measuring the exact degree of excitement which, bordering on exasperation, feels almost overcharged and can only stagnate? From the fact that it won't be that position that gives me the impression of being satisfied by my

imaginary partner?) that, if I carry on, I won't get to orgasm or, if I do, it won't be very intense. So I stop the movement abruptly and backtrack in my story. I lick a few stiffened dicks before choosing one. Back to the massage table. (There can be multiple flashbacks, each one slightly different.) This time there are two or three who will take it in turns in my cunt. I increase the pressure with my finger, my clitoris rolls over a firm base, a bone? I picture one of the boys hammering me. The friction becomes frenetic. I sometimes murmur a few basic words of encouragement, pronouncing the words quite clearly: 'You're so good,' 'Go on . . .' When the time comes, my mind empties. Exit the fifteen stallions. I grimace with concentration, curl my mouth up in an ugly snarl; one of my legs becomes paralysed but, in an unexpected switch, I sometimes spontaneously knead one of my breasts gently with my free hand. The orgasm comes as the result of a decision. If I can put it like this: I can see it coming. In fact, I often really do have my eyes wide open, and they don't see the wall in front of me or the ceiling, but a fantasy X-ray. If it has gone well, the pleasure comes from far away, from the very depths of that long gut, with its ridged, grey walls, right to the mouth which opens and closes like the jaw of a fish. Every other muscle relaxes. There can be six or seven waves. Ideally, I stay there for a moment sliding my fingers over my vulva, then I bring them up to my nose to revel in the sweetish smell. I don't wash my hands.

I masturbate with the regularity of a civil servant. When I wake, or during the day, with my back up against a wall, my legs spread and slightly bent, never at night. I take just as much pleasure in doing it when I am well shafted for

real. In those instances, it takes me longer to come; I find it more difficult concentrating on my fantasy narrative, because the organ lodged inside me does not exclude the one I imagine. The real one stands ready, motionless and patient until I give the signal, a 'yeh' of total acquiescence or a toss of my head, and the spasms that I have provoked meet the charges of the penis at its most powerful. Can I really be bringing together two such very different forms of pleasure, the one that is felt so distinctly that I can almost feel my internal space expanding in the same way that I would watch the tide rising over the beach, and the other far more diffuse pleasure, as if my body were reverberating like a muted gong because, like when we suffer extreme pain, the mind distances itself from it?

I have never identified the contractions of my vagina when making love. I have remained completely ignorant on that subject. Is it because I don't recognise that sort of orgasm in those circumstances? Is it because, filled by my partner's organ, my own does not have the same elasticity? Still, happily, I did eventually realise that it was one manifestation of the female orgasm. I was over thirty when a male friend and I had one of those intimate conversations which are very rare in life. He was worrying about how one could tell when a woman had come. 'Is it when she has spasms? Is that the only proof?' he asked me. Hesitantly, but not wanting to look a fool, I said yes. I kept to myself the fact that I was thinking: 'so that's what it is.' Until then, when my body had emitted these sorts of signals, I had not identified them as such, even if it was while I was masturbating with the precision I have described. Having not knowingly striven for the thing they signified, I could not recognise them as signs. Some

caresses made me feel good, some positions were better than others, and that was it. I now understand that that laconic conversation (with a man – and this is not a co-incidence – with whom I hadn't had a sexual relationship) must have sown in me the seed of an anxiety which took many long years to develop into the state of dissatisfaction which came up at the end of the first chapter of this book.

As I have also explained, for me masturbation was initially, and for a long time, not a question of addressing the clitoris directly, but of sliding the lips of the vulva against each other. It wasn't that I didn't know it existed, it was that I hadn't needed to worry about it in order to experience my pleasure. I belong to the generation of women targeted by feminist books with the aim of guiding them in the exploration of their own bodies. I have squatted on a mirror and looked at my genitals, but that only confused me. Perhaps I found it difficult to follow a very scientific description. Perhaps I was slightly prejudiced against the feminists' approach which I thought was intended for women who were inhibited or were experiencing difficulties in their sexual relationships, which didn't include me because, for me, fucking was easy. Perhaps I didn't want to call this easiness into question: Yes, I fucked for the pleasure of it, but didn't I also fuck so that fucking wasn't a problem? Perhaps on that occasion I closed my thighs the way you would close a medical dictionary: for fear of finding in yourself the illnesses they describe which would preclude you from some very enjoyable habits . . .

I was absolutely right because when, much later, I opened the dictionary of received wisdom, my worries started to well up. At that stage I had a relationship with

216

one man, and then a second, and I got it into my head that I should feel the same spasms when I was making love to them as I did when I was masturbating. Was I sufficiently familiar with my own organs to achieve this? And, as if my sexual life were happening in reverse, as if I had to ask myself the naive questions after acquiring and then forgetting all my experience, I was full of doubt about my clitoral antenna. Did it respond when I aroused myself with a manic finger? For a while I thought I didn't have one or that it had atrophied. A man with the best intentions but nevertheless not very adept, and whose finger kept missing the mark, didn't help. Eventually I cottoned on: the clitoris was not an obvious landmark like a nail on a wall, a steeple in a landscape or a nose on a face, it was a sort of muddled knot, with no true shape, a minute chaos where two little tongues of flesh meet like when a backwash throws two waves together.

Pleasure taken alone can be told, pleasure taken with another is elusive. Unlike when I bring about my own orgasm, when I am with someone else I never say: 'This is it.' No defining moment, no flash. Rather a slow settling into a mellow state of pure sensation. The opposite of a local anaesthetic which suppresses sensitivity but allows you to remain conscious: I am cut to the quick and my entire body becomes the rim of this laceration, while my mind reaches out to a sleep-like state. Even though I can still move, it is only on auto-pilot, still able to utter a final social grace: 'Does it matter if I don't move any more?' Is that fulfilment? It is more like the state we reach shortly before passing out, when we feel as if the body is emptying itself. Invaded, yes, but by emptiness. I feel cold like when the blood ebbs away. It flows downwards. A

valve has opened and through it I am losing everything that made my body a compact mass. And I can hear the noise of this expulsion. Every time the member renews its advance within the soft pocket that I have become, the displaced air emits a clear sound. It is a while now since I gave up screaming, since I woke the neighbours' baby and they complained by banging on the wall. The friend I was with was annoyed and he called me a few days later to inform me that: 'I've spoken to a doctor friend about it; screaming like that is a sign of hysteria.' I got over the habit without even noticing. Since then, other women's screams have often reminded me of those cries – more deliberate than spontaneous – made by horseback riders to encourage their mounts as they hurtle past you in the ring. All I give out now are farts. The first one catches me by surprise as I drowsily luxuriate. Others follow. I am amazed at my largesse.

Would the doctor friend have qualified or corrected his diagnosis had he known that, for a while, when my partners abandoned me on the bed, the table or the floor after making love, they left a body that was as stiff as a corpse? Luckily, it wasn't like that every time, but, as far as I can remember, when the pleasure had been intense, my muscles would go into spasm. I was never frightened. It didn't last long. The same symptoms occurred once when I had an abortion, and the gynaecologist said that I was lacking in calcium. It wasn't even painful. It just happened like proof that something incomprehensible had happened in my body, which no longer belonged to me. The paralysis prolonged my lethargy. I obviously wondered whether, as well as the salt deficiency, there wasn't also some subconscious motivation. Was I holding

back my body before or after orgasm? To avoid it or to prolong it? The symptom disappeared and I forgot to answer the question. Then the opposite sort of behaviour occurred. Instead of tensing when on the edge of the abyss, I would drown in my own tears. I would let go of all my tension with noisy, uninhibited sobs. I cried in a way you hardly ever do in adult life, the heart filled with sorrow. The tension had to be particularly high, exceptional even; perhaps more so than other women, I have a long way to go to reach ecstasy, and my tears are a little like those of an exhausted athlete awarded their first medal. A few of my partners were terrified, they were afraid they had hurt me. But they were tears of hopeless joy. I had jettisoned everything, but all that everything was only this: the body I had offered was just a breath of air, and the one I held and kissed was already light years away. So utterly destitute, how could I not express my distress?

Even the most violent onslaughts don't get the better of me. You have to absorb the shocks, and when I end up with the small of my back crushed down onto the mattress, I feel too weighty for any form of Ascension. When I am well prepared I prefer certain tiny adjustments which conversely imply that I weigh nothing. A brief gesture from one particular man struck me as quite divine; he was much taller than me, and he would gently drum his fingers in the small of my back. His attentiveness was so well honed as to be mechanical: the housewife doing her dusting. Three or four sharp little taps and I rose into the air like a sheet of paper in a draught. It made my cunt take in another few millimetres of his cock. It was enough.

The Sexual Life of Catherine M.

Viewing

I am of average height and I have a supple body, you can catch hold of me and turn me every which way. What surprises me the most when I see myself on a video screen is this malleability. I usually feel so ill-at-ease, so awkward (I have hardly danced since my adolescence, and I couldn't swim more than three strokes in the sea), that I don't recognise this inoffensive reptile stretching, retracting and reacting swiftly and completely to every demand. Lying on my side in an odalisque's pose, with my legs slightly bent to bring the curve of my buttocks into the foreground, my gaze turned in the same direction that this curve is offered, my hand open on my mouth as I wait to see what will happen. Then, still on my side, but curled a little more tightly to offer a better grip, my waist twisted a quarter turn to the back, making my upper body stand out, and my neck turned so that I can at a glance check that the slit is visible. In that position I can do little. The animal pretends to be an inanimate object. The man bends my legs a little further so that he can wedge one of his in the triangle they form; he looks as if he is gathering up a parcel to make it easier to pick up. He keeps them bent with a firm hand and shakes the object in front of him violently so that it springs supply back against his belly. I like this state of inertia even though when my sex is penetrated from the side like this it is not very receptive. It is the same when the man comes to lie down on his side forming the bar of a T for which I, having turned back onto my back, form the downstroke, with one of my legs lying over his waist and the other over his thighs. Again I take on an animal identity, somewhere between a frog and

those upside-down insects that beat the air with their short legs. As I have said, I do, however, prefer to be taken from the front. I feel each ram of the dick more clearly and I can regain some understanding of what is going on. By lifting my head and, if need be, holding up my ankles or my calves, I can watch what's happening framed between my wide-apart legs. I can take the initiative: arching my back, for example, to raise my hips and moving them as much as possible. The relationship between the elements is reversed: it is no longer a stake driving into the earth, but the earth quaking to swallow it up. On the flat again. Pulled onto my back like a dead weight, I become objectified once more. Later, on the screen, I will see myself taking on the shape of an upside down vase. The base is my knees which I have brought up to my face, my thighs are squeezed up to my trunk forming a cone which gets wider as it reaches the buttocks and then narrows at the neck after flaring widely on each side – would that be the curve of the iliac bones? – leaving just enough room for the plunging rod.

The pleasure is only fleeting because the body so pummelled, prodded and manhandled is evanescent. The body which has reached orgasm has been as completely absorbed into deep, mysterious recesses as the body of a pianist is concentrated in the tips of his fingers. And do the pianist's fingers put any weight on the keys? At times, it doesn't seem so. Watching a video in which I masturbate with a floating hand, the man next to me says I look like a guitar player. My fingers are relaxed and they swing backwards and forwards in the dark cloud like clockwork, but their movements are very precise. When I am not alone and I know that they will soon be replaced by a

much bigger instrument, I never press too hard, I make the most of this sweetness. I never masturbate by inserting my fingers into my cunt, I make do with barely dipping in my middle finger in order to moisten the front. If the movements become a bit more pronounced, the fine skin on the inside of the thighs is rippled by a wave. I see that I am gently touching my partner's organ in the same way. As I get down to a blow-job, I protect the bottom of his penis and his testicles in the crook of my hands in exactly the same way that I would gather a lizard or a bird. One close-up shows me with my mouth full and my eyes wide open looking at the screen; there is a degree of technical control in this gaze. In another, my eyes and mouth are closed, with the latter offered to the glans which explores it; I look as if I am sound asleep when I am actually concentrating hard to stay in focus. Later, wanting to take in the glans, I carefully open and push aside the labia, well aware of how fragile this object that I am about to wrap myself round is.

Another film shows the whole of my body, behaving as it never would dressed, as I carry out my normal day-to-day tasks. Jacques, the director, makes me go up and down the stairs of our building twenty times in a dress of transparent black linen (there aren't many people on the stairs at that time of day). As if I were wearing a normal, opaque dress and was being followed by an X-ray camera, you can make out from behind the pneumatic animation of the buttocks, and, from in front, you can see the trembling in my breasts each time one of my feet comes down on a step, while my pubic hair disappears into a wide shadow when it rubs up against the cloth. Even though my flesh has density, the silhouette is transient.

For the next sequence, Jacques asks me to stand in the little shelter where the concierge works during the day, firstly with the top of the dress rolled down to my waist and then without the dress, and he asks me to adopt the various poses of the job. Oh, if only you could leave home and go to work with nothing on like that! It wouldn't only be the weight of the clothes we would be freed from, it would also be the heaviness of the body which they would take with them. I admit it: the role that Jacques makes me play coincides so precisely with my own fantasies that I am unusually disturbed, almost embarrassed to find myself more naked than naked. We go back into the apartment. There, by contrast, my body stands out very clearly against the white sofa. In the middle the hand comes and goes slowly, weighed down by a huge ring, and it is only the intermittent glinting of this ring that compromises the clarity of the image. My thighs and legs are spread wide inscribing an almost perfect square. That is what I see today, but at the time I knew that it was what the man behind the camera was seeing. When, without putting the camera down, he came to remove my hand, my organ in which he slid his was as tumescent as never before. The reason was immediately clear: I was already filled by the coincidence of my real body and these multiple, volatile images.

A SELECTED LIST OF NON-FICTION TITLES
AVAILABLE FROM CORGI AND BANTAM BOOKS

09806 X	WHAT DO YOU SAY AFTER YOU SAY HELLO?	Eric Berne M.D.	£6.99
81487 7	THE BOOK OF LOVE ANSWERS	Carol Bolt	£9.99
14707 9	HOT SEX	Tracey Cox	£7.99
14784 2	HOT RELATIONSHIPS	Tracey Cox	£8.99
14956 X	HOT SEX POCKET EDITION	Tracey Cox	£4.99
14955 1	HOT LOVE POCKET EDITION	Tracey Cox	£4.99
14938 1	THE FABULOUS GIRL'S GUIDE TO DECORUM	Kim Izzo & Ceri Marsh	£6.99
81475 3	THE GOOD GIRL'S GUIDE TO BAD GIRL SEX	Barbara Keesling PhD	£6.99
15025 8	I WAS A TEENAGE DOMINATRIX	Shawna Kenney	£5.99
81526 1	THE SOUL OF SEX	Thomas Moore	£7.99
08930 3	STORY OF O	Pauline Reage	£6.99
12571 7	STORY OF O PART II	Pauline Reage	£5.99
50473 8	203 WAYS TO DRIVE A MAN WILD IN BED	Olivia St Claire	£5.99
50485 1	227 WAYS TO UNLEASH THE SEX GODDESS IN EVERY WOMAN	Olivia St Claire	£5.99
81473 7	302 ADVANCED TECHNIQUES FOR DRIVING A MAN WILD IN BED	Olivia St Claire	£6.99
50579 3	THE FRAGRANT HEAVENS	Valerie Ann Worwood	£8.99
14973 X	MOUTH MUSIC MADE EASY	Harry and Caddie Youngberry	£3.99

'This is the most explicit book about sex ever written by a woman, though it is far from pornographic. Catherine Millet sets about coolly and rationally exploring her insatiable appetites – and she has lived to tell the tale that is the opposite of lurid. It is a comprehensive and elegant performance'
Edmund White

'Keeps crudeness at bay through an aloof, gracefully crystalline style as elegant as any French pornography since Sade'
Vogue (USA)

'This stylistic tour de force recounting three decades of sexual exploits surprises not only because it is from a woman's point of view but because it avoids politics altogether . . . Millet refuses to serve up a social morality tale . . . Hers is the revenge of sex on politics . . . For Millet autobiography seems, rather, to be a tale of living – quite literally – in the body. If that's the case, then reading this book may be less a matter of finding in it an exemplary life, or even a mirror for oneself. It's merely a matter of assuming the correct position. Relax, sit back, and enjoy'
Bookforum

'It is Millet's subversive achievement to describe pleasure for its own sake'
New Statesman

'The graceful, thoughtful, oddly charming, and pro-foundly pornographic account of a French intellectual's life of extreme sexuality . . . In a translation that preserves the elegance and clarity of Millet's prose, we are launched almost immediately into her life of group sex, anonymous sex, serial and public sex . . . will surely be the most blatantly pornographic read many will encounter this year . . . A bold, intelligent, pioneering tour de force'
Kirkus Reviews

KT-495-365

Catherine Millet, who lives in Paris, is an expert on modern art and is the editor of the magazine, *Art Press*. Her last book, *L'Art Contemporain*, was published in 1997. She curated the French section of the 1989 Sao Paulo Biennale and the French Pavilion at the 1995 Venice Biennale.